# 1,003
# Great Things
# About Being
# *Jewish*

## Other Books by Lisa Birnbach

*1,003 Great Things About America*
*1,003 Great Things About Moms*
*1,003 Great Things About Teachers*
*1,003 Great Things About Friends*
*1,003 Great Things About Kids*
*1,003 Great Things About Getting Older*
*1,003 Great Things to Smile About*
*1,003 Great Things About Being a Woman*
*The Official Preppy Handbook*
*Lisa Birnbach College Books*
*Going to Work*
*Loose Lips*

## Other Books by Ann Hodgman

*1,003 Great Things About America*
*1,003 Great Things About Moms*
*1,003 Great Things About Teachers*
*1,003 Great Things About Friends*
*1,003 Great Things About Kids*
*1,003 Great Things About Getting Older*
*1,003 Great Things to Smile About*
*1,003 Great Things About Being a Woman*
*My Babysitter Is a Vampire* (series)
*Beat This!*
*Beat That!*
*One Bite Won't Kill You*
*I Saw Mommy Kicking Santa Claus*

# 1,003
# Great Things
# About Being
## Jewish

Lisa Birnbach, Ann Hodgman,
Polly Stone

**Andrews McMeel
Publishing**

Kansas City

06 07 08 09 10 BID 10 9 8 7 6 5 4 3 2 1


ISBN-13: 978-0-7407-5529-3

ISBN-10: 0-7407-5529-3


Library of Congress Control Number: 2005932599


www.andrewsmcmeel.com

# 1,003
# Great Things
# About Being
# Jewish

*L'chaim!*

*Shalom* means hello, good-bye, and peace, and that's a lot for a word.

From a safe distance in time, the old Lower East Side sounds sort of picturesque.

A *yad* is the pointer used to read the Torah. Isn't that a great word?

Traditional Jewish cuisine makes
excellent use of poppy seeds.

You're not supposed to mow the lawn
on the Sabbath. Whew!

(Better not clean the hamster cage, either,
just to be on the safe side.)

However, all Sabbath prohibitions
may be violated in order to save a life.

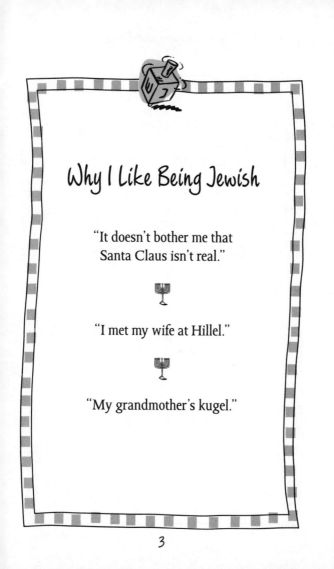

# Why I Like Being Jewish

"It doesn't bother me that
Santa Claus isn't real."

"I met my wife at Hillel."

"My grandmother's kugel."

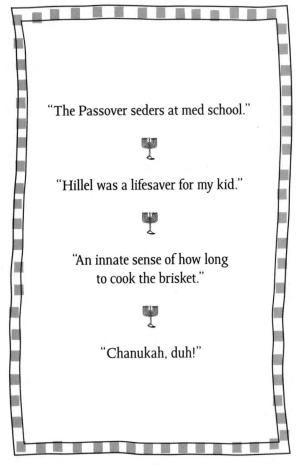

"The Passover seders at med school."

"Hillel was a lifesaver for my kid."

"An innate sense of how long
to cook the brisket."

"Chanukah, duh!"

"Taking my kids and my parents
to see *Fiddler on the Roof.*"

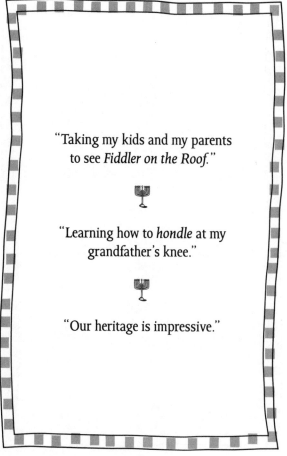

"Learning how to *hondle* at my
grandfather's knee."

"Our heritage is impressive."

"The raid at Entebbe was a proud moment."

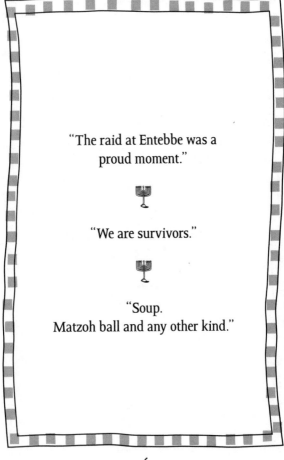

"We are survivors."

"Soup.
Matzoh ball and any other kind."

You can order your *succah* online.

Elvis Presley's great-great-grandmother
was Jewish.

Did you hear about the Jewish family that
kept such a kosher kitchen, they had two
smoke detectors over the stove?

Sarah's prophetic skills were
greater than Abraham's.

God gave the Jews not just one,
but two covenants.

✡

You're *supposed* to drink alcohol on Purim.

✡

In addition to everything else he had going on,
Moses found time to write the Pentateuch.

✡

It's getting to be more fashionable
among Christians to call the Hebrew Bible
the "First Testament" instead of the
"Old Testament."

# Ten Commandments for the New Millennium

## I

I am the Lord thy God. Thou shalt have no other gods before me, save only for thine offspring's independent college counselor.

## II

Thou shalt not make unto thee any graven image, or any likeness of anything that is in heaven above, or that is in the earth beneath, or that is in the water under the earth. However, thou shalt feel free to disregard the "earth" and "water under the earth" parts, as no one except thy God hath any idea where Moses was going with those.

### III

Thou shalt not take the name of the Lord thy God in vain, but a little cursing is okay if thou art on the turnpike behind a driver in the left lane who driveth at 40 mph.

### IV

Thou shalt remember the Sabbath and keep it holy by playing golf, hanging out at the mall, doing the crossword puzzle, catching up on thy e-mail, taking thy clothes to the cleaners, throwing a dinner party, seeing a movie at the cineplex, dining at the latest bistro, watching television, and complaining about work.

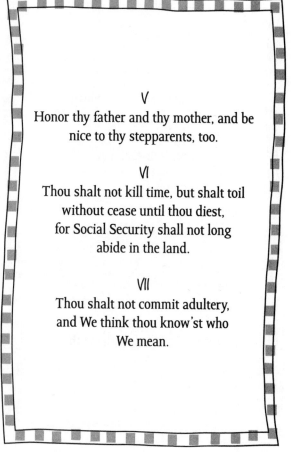

V

Honor thy father and thy mother, and be
nice to thy stepparents, too.

VI

Thou shalt not kill time, but shalt toil
without cease until thou diest,
for Social Security shall not long
abide in the land.

VII

Thou shalt not commit adultery,
and We think thou know'st who
We mean.

VIII
Thou shalt not steal, which
includeth faithfully reporting all
thy income and not taking
undue deductions.

IX
Thou shalt not bear false witness except
when thou sayest dinner tastes
great when surely it doth not.

X
Thou shalt not covet thy neighbor's house,
because dost thou know
how big a mortgage he hath?

"Jewry" is just two letters away
from "jewelry."

"Jewish road trip" = Driving to the airport.

It is not required that your dentist
give you kosher fillings.

This year, the rabbi's Yom Kippur
speech was actually new!

Leaf through a Bible if you want to find
a lot of different ways to describe sex
("knowing," "lying with," "consorting").

"Being fruitful" probably counts, too.

And let's not forget "dwelling with."

And "took."

And "had relations."

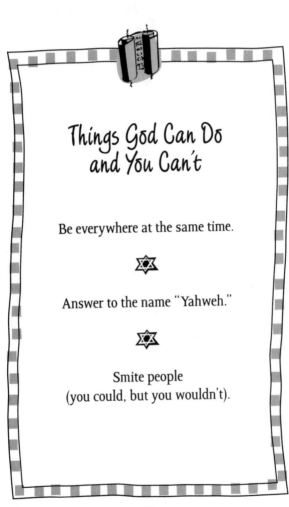

# Things God Can Do and You Can't

Be everywhere at the same time.

✡

Answer to the name "Yahweh."

✡

Smite people
(you could, but you wouldn't).

Create the universe.

✡

Create Eve out of a rib.

✡

Establish a covenant with
the Jewish people.

Argue with the Devil.

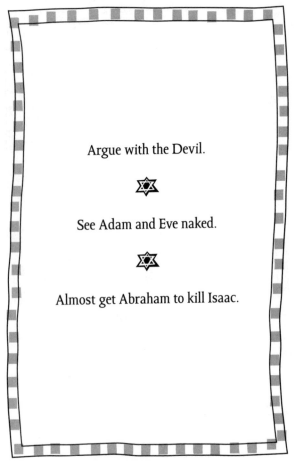

See Adam and Eve naked.

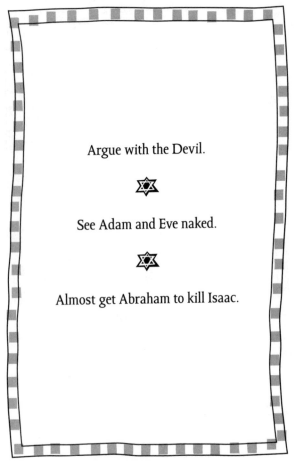

Almost get Abraham to kill Isaac.

Send us His only begotten Son that we should not perish but have eternal life— oh, sorry, wrong religion.

✡

Turn someone into a pillar of salt.

✡

Inspire psalms.

Have His name invoked every
time someone sneezes.

✡

Have the whole world in His hands.

✡

Cause thunder and lightning.

Make rainbows.

Part the Red Sea.

Un-part it right afterward.

Turn Mom's hair gray.

# Things God Can Do and So Can You!

Feel wrath.

✡

Show mercy.

✡

Forbear.

Change His mind.

Give and take away.

Create life.

Annoy life.

Start a forest fire (please don't).

✡

Feed the fish.

✡

Admire His creations.

✡

Flood an anthill.

Ignore prayers.

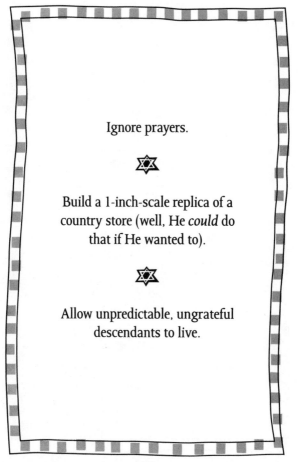

Build a 1-inch-scale replica of a country store (well, He *could* do that if He wanted to).

✡

Allow unpredictable, ungrateful descendants to live.

Let there be light.

Rest on the seventh day.

Turn Mom's hair gray.

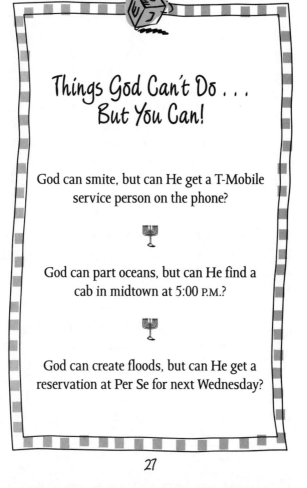

# Things God Can't Do . . .
## But You Can!

God can smite, but can He get a T-Mobile
service person on the phone?

God can part oceans, but can He find a
cab in midtown at 5:00 P.M.?

God can create floods, but can He get a
reservation at Per Se for next Wednesday?

God can lead the Jews into the
Promised Land, but can He get a room at
Cap Juluca over Christmas vacation?

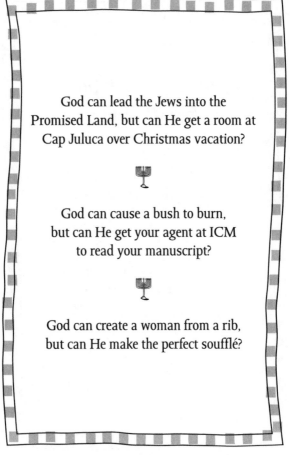

God can cause a bush to burn,
but can He get your agent at ICM
to read your manuscript?

God can create a woman from a rib,
but can He make the perfect soufflé?

God can perform a miracle, but can He figure out how to program my iPod?

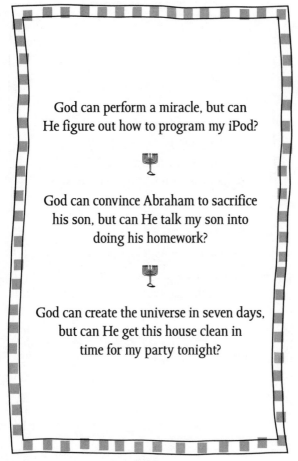

God can convince Abraham to sacrifice his son, but can He talk my son into doing his homework?

God can create the universe in seven days, but can He get this house clean in time for my party tonight?

God can sanctify, but can He find anything nice to say about the addition the Temelmans just put on their house?

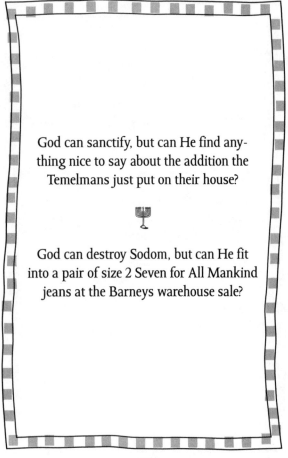

God can destroy Sodom, but can He fit into a pair of size 2 Seven for All Mankind jeans at the Barneys warehouse sale?

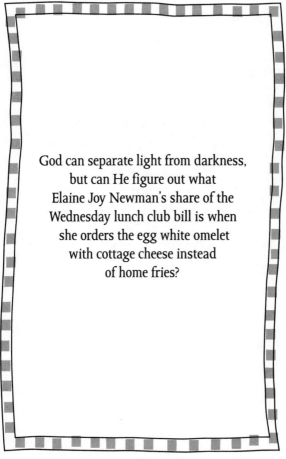

God can separate light from darkness,
but can He figure out what
Elaine Joy Newman's share of the
Wednesday lunch club bill is when
she orders the egg white omelet
with cottage cheese instead
of home fries?

All Jewish folktales seem to involve
shoemakers, the rabbi's apprentice,
and a beggar who turns out to be Elijah.

No one expects you to win a marathon.

Margie Munter puts dried
cranberries in her kugel!

In Israel, Friday the thirteenth
is considered lucky.

✡

Barry Glick is standing at the counter of
his favorite gourmet store. "I'll have a pound
of that salmon," he orders. "That isn't salmon;
it's ham," corrects the clerk. "Mister,"
snaps Glick, "in case nobody ever told you,
you got a big mouth!"

"Roses are reddish,
Violets are bluish,
If it weren't for Christmas,
Everyone would be Jewish."

✡

Two Jewish men, Joel and Arthur Spingarn,
helped found the National Association for the
Advancement of Colored People.

Jewish organizations such as the American Jewish Committee and the American Jewish Congress were key players in the campaign against racism.

Williamsburg in Brooklyn is getting to be a really hip neighborhood.

My, that movie *Crossing Delancey* was sweet.

## Cool Things About Israel

Natalie Portman was born there!

✡

Every Jewish citizen of Israel is entitled
to a free burial plot.

✡

In 1984 and 1991, Israel airlifted to safety
in Israel a total of twenty-two thousand
Ethiopian Jews at risk in Ethiopia.

The Israeli Army serves only kosher food.

Primate research at Hebrew University is leading to the development of a robotic arm that can respond to the brain commands of a paralyzed person.

Israeli researchers developed a stem cell therapy to treat Parkinson's disease.

The Israeli company Silent
Communications has developed a type of
silent conversation system for cell phones,
so users can carry on conversations
without saying a word.

✡

Israeli professor Yehuda Finkelstein
has discovered the cause of
and cure for halitosis.

✡

Cherry tomatoes were designed by a
group of Israeli scientists.

An Israeli company developed "The
Quicktionary," a pen-size scanner that
scans a word or a sentence and translates
it to a different language.

✡

Professor Ehud Keinan from the
Technion Israel Institute of Technology
developed a pen that identifies an
improvised explosive.

The Israeli company Insightec developed
an ultrasound system for removing
tumors without surgery.

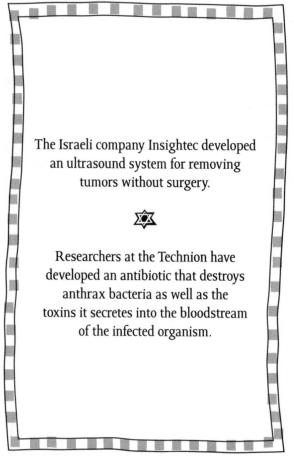

Researchers at the Technion have
developed an antibiotic that destroys
anthrax bacteria as well as the
toxins it secretes into the bloodstream
of the infected organism.

Epilady, an electric hair removal system,
was developed in Israel.

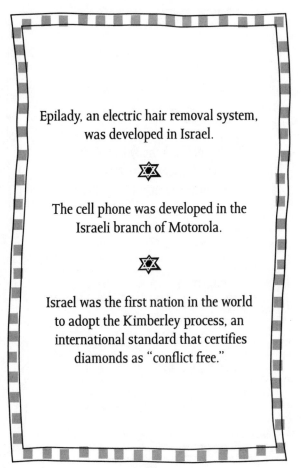

The cell phone was developed in the
Israeli branch of Motorola.

Israel was the first nation in the world
to adopt the Kimberley process, an
international standard that certifies
diamonds as "conflict free."

Israel leads the world in the
number of scientists and technicians
in the workforce, with 145 per
10,000 (as opposed to 85
in the United States).

With over 25 percent of its workforce
employed in technical professions, Israel
places first in this category as well.

A new acne treatment developed in Israel, the ClearLight device, produces a high-intensity, ultraviolet-light-free, narrow-band blue light that causes acne bacteria to self-destruct—without damaging surrounding skin or tissue.

Relative to its population, Israel is the largest immigrant-absorbing nation on earth.

Israel has the world's second highest per capita purchase of new books.

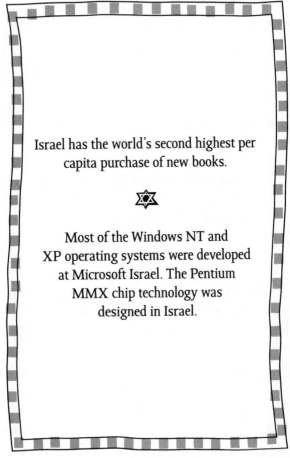

Most of the Windows NT and XP operating systems were developed at Microsoft Israel. The Pentium MMX chip technology was designed in Israel.

Both the Pentium 4 microprocessor and the Centrino processor were entirely designed, developed, and produced in Israel.

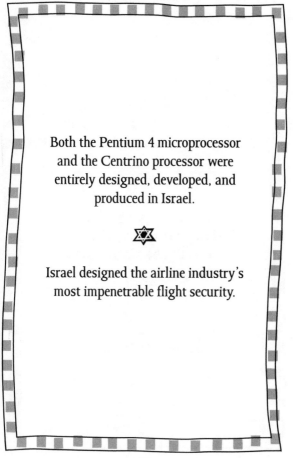

Israel designed the airline industry's most impenetrable flight security.

An Israeli Company, Givun Imaging, created the first ingestible video camera. The camera is so small it fits inside a pill.

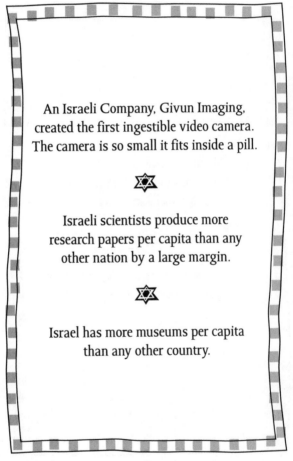

Israeli scientists produce more research papers per capita than any other nation by a large margin.

Israel has more museums per capita than any other country.

Israel is the only country in the
world that entered the twenty-first century
with a net gain in its number of trees—
pretty amazing in a country with
so much desert.

Israeli scientists developed the first fully
computerized, no-radiation, diagnostic
instrumentation for breast cancer.

Israeli law forbids picking your
nose on the Sabbath.

An Israeli company developed a computerized system for ensuring proper administration of medications, thus removing human error from medical treatment.

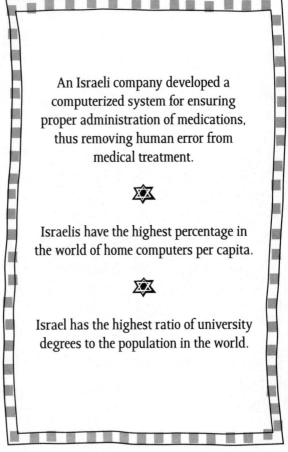

Israelis have the highest percentage in the world of home computers per capita.

Israel has the highest ratio of university degrees to the population in the world.

Israel has the third highest rate of
entrepreneurship—and the highest
rate among women and among people
over fifty-five—in the world.

Israel is ranked second in the world for
venture capital funds.

Israel has the sixteenth highest life
expectancy in the world
(ahead of the United States).

In 1952, Albert Einstein was offered the presidency of Israel . . . which he declined.

✡

Dror Orpaz and Carmit Tsubara kissed for thirty hours and forty-five minutes in Tel Aviv in 1999, setting a world record.

✡

"The air of the land of Israel makes one wise." —Talmud

We are more likely to have a Jewish president in this country than, say, a Ba'hai president.

Or a transgendered president.

We are good and faithful supporters of public broadcasting.

We love NPR.

Someone out there has crocheted yarmulkes
with every imaginable major sports franchise
logo on them.

And we've even seen suede yarmulkes with
Big Bird and Elmo painted on them.

The Noga Hilton in Cannes, France, makes its
kitchen kosher for Passover.

And there are kosher cruises, too.

We have some openly gay
Jewish congregations . . .

. . . With openly gay rabbis.

We are so open-minded that when the neo-Nazis
wanted to march in Skokie, Illinois, a Jewish
ACLU lawyer tried to defend them.

The people down the street named their basset hound Job, because he has such a sad face.

If David can kill Goliath, then you can empty the mousetrap.

It is possible to have a Talmudic discussion about the advantages of wearing heels versus flat shoes.

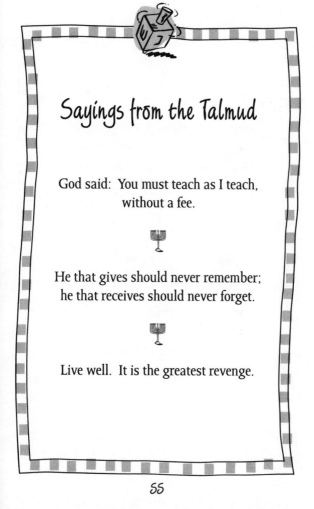

# Sayings from the Talmud

God said:  You must teach as I teach,
without a fee.

He that gives should never remember;
he that receives should never forget.

Live well.  It is the greatest revenge.

Never expose yourself unnecessarily to
danger; a miracle may not save you . . .
and if it does, it will be deducted from
your share of luck or merit.

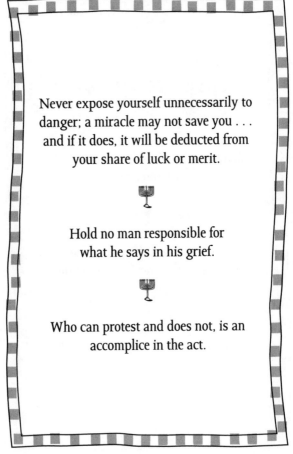

Hold no man responsible for
what he says in his grief.

Who can protest and does not, is an
accomplice in the act.

Whoever destroys a single life is as guilty
as though he had destroyed the entire
world; and whoever rescues a single
life earns as much merit as though he had
rescued the entire world.

Man has three friends on whom he relies:
First, wealth, which goes with him as
long as good fortune lasts. Second,
his relatives, who go only as far as
the grave and leave him there. The third
friend, his good deeds, goes with him
beyond the grave.

When love is strong, a man and a woman
can make their bed on a sword's blade.
When love is weak, a bed of sixty cubits
is not large enough.

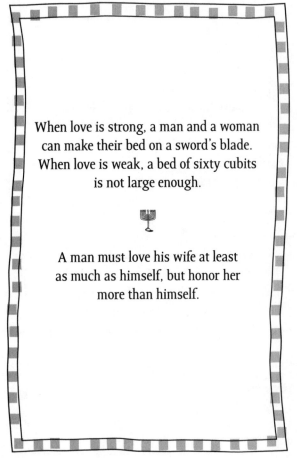

A man must love his wife at least
as much as himself, but honor her
more than himself.

Beware of too much laughter, for it deadens the mind and produces oblivion.

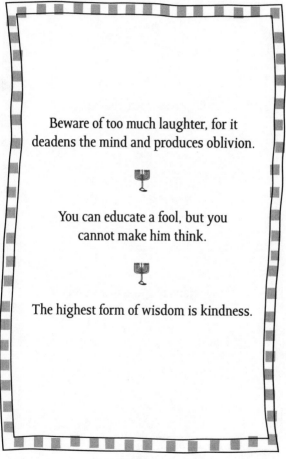

You can educate a fool, but you cannot make him think.

The highest form of wisdom is kindness.

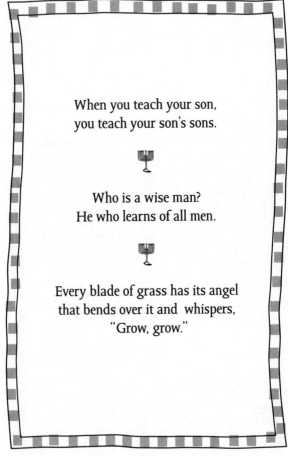

When you teach your son,
you teach your son's sons.

Who is a wise man?
He who learns of all men.

Every blade of grass has its angel
that bends over it and whispers,
"Grow, grow."

Nobody seems to notice how many sandwiches
you take at the Kiddush.

✡

Doesn't the custom of answering a question with a
question mean you never have to know anything?

✡

In addition to being a great prophetess, Deborah
made the wicks for the candles in the Temple, to
encourage study of the Torah.

"Tzitzit" is a much better word than "strings."

We don't skimp on the cream cheese.

Kosher-for-Passover Coca-Cola is made with cane sugar instead of corn syrup.
Stock up for the rest of the year—it tastes better than the corn-syrup kind!

# The Worst Places to Hide the Afikoman

Under the Easter eggs.

In Grandpa's stomach.

Under Grandma's wig.

In the liquor cabinet.

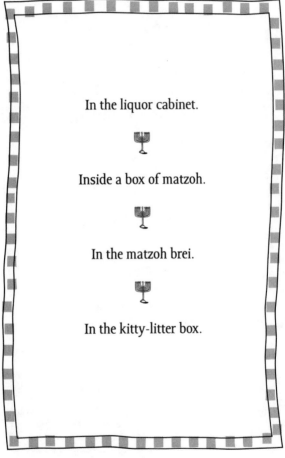

Inside a box of matzoh.

In the matzoh brei.

In the kitty-litter box.

In the new and improved
Afikoman-a-Hider™.

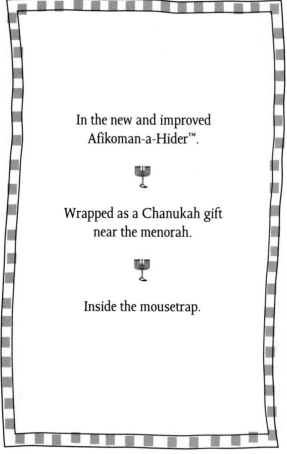

Wrapped as a Chanukah gift
near the menorah.

Inside the mousetrap.

Underneath the brisket.

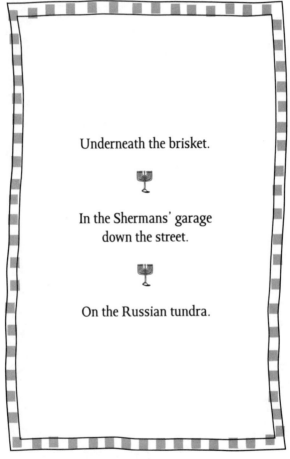

In the Shermans' garage
down the street.

On the Russian tundra.

Like lighting candles?
Then the Sabbath is for you!
(Also, Chanukah.)

There is a Hebrew blessing for when the
sun aligns with the earth.

Moshe Dayan could do more with one eye
than most people could do with two.

Lizanne passed notes to her
friends in Hebrew School class inside her
teacher's wide-legged cuffs!

"The remarkable thing about my mother
is that for thirty years, she served nothing
but leftovers. The original meal has never
been found." —Calvin Trillin

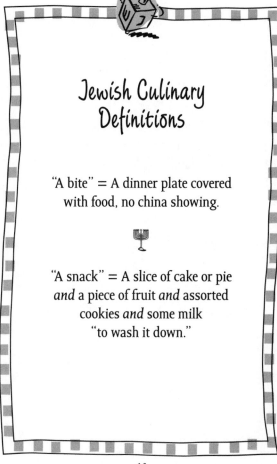

# Jewish Culinary Definitions

"A bite" = A dinner plate covered
with food, no china showing.

"A snack" = A slice of cake or pie
*and* a piece of fruit *and* assorted
cookies *and* some milk
"to wash it down."

"A smidgeon" = Half a roast chicken
*or* an oversized sandwich *or*
a full tureen of soup.

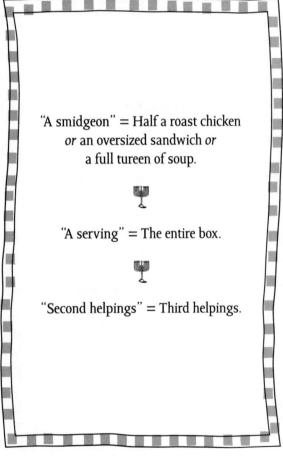

"A serving" = The entire box.

"Second helpings" = Third helpings.

"A diet" = Limiting yourself to one meal per meal.

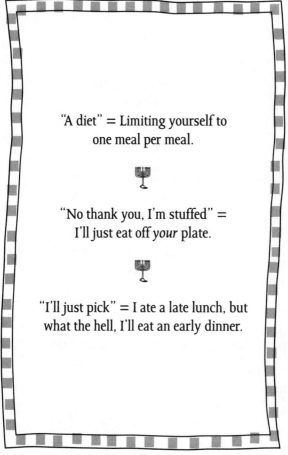

"No thank you, I'm stuffed" = I'll just eat off *your* plate.

"I'll just pick" = I ate a late lunch, but what the hell, I'll eat an early dinner.

"You eat like a bird" = You're making me feel self-conscious.

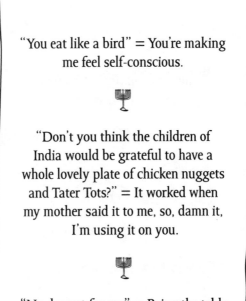

"Don't you think the children of India would be grateful to have a whole lovely plate of chicken nuggets and Tater Tots?" = It worked when my mother said it to me, so, damn it, I'm using it on you.

"No dessert for me" = Bring the table one of each and put them in front of me.

We're not into witches or ghosts.

Bruriah is celebrated for having learned
three hundred Jewish laws a day.

According to an old Israeli superstition,
if someone wants to keep bees away,
he should say "salt and water."

Ehud Barak, former prime minister of Israel,
played Beethoven's "Moonlight Sonata"
on the piano in a TV show.

Cain and Abel invented sibling rivalry.

Who *wants* to eat pork, anyway?

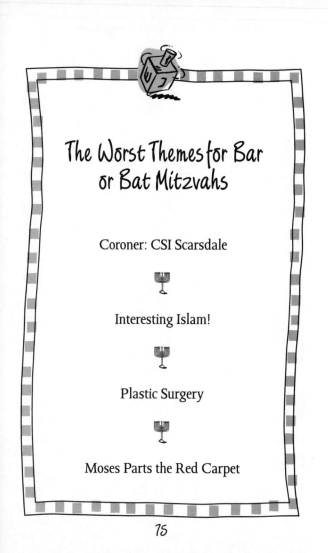

# The Worst Themes for Bar or Bat Mitzvahs

Coroner: CSI Scarsdale

Interesting Islam!

Plastic Surgery

Moses Parts the Red Carpet

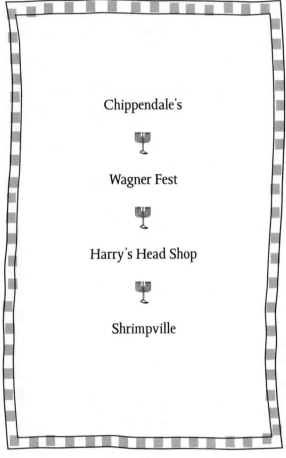

Chippendale's

Wagner Fest

Harry's Head Shop

Shrimpville

Dance with Your Dad

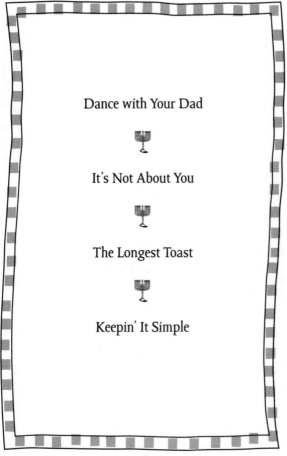

It's Not About You

The Longest Toast

Keepin' It Simple

Let's Help Jacob Write
His Thank-You Notes

Fiddler on the Terrace

Noah's Yacht: The Cruise

Silent Night, Holy Night

If you name your daughter "Holly," you can tell your grandparents that she's named after challah.

Some people are kosher at home but eat shrimp cocktail at restaurants.

Soy cheese allows you to eat cheeseburgers . . . finally.

If you don't get into the opera company, you could consider studying to be a cantor.

✡

A prayer shawl looks like an opera scarf, anyway.

✡

If you're bored during services, you can try braiding the fringe of a tallith (prayer shawl).

But it would be better to braid your daddy's shawl, not a stranger's.

By the time you've attended about fifteen Rosh Hashanah services, you pretty much know the melodies by heart.

And they haven't changed in over five thousand years.

# How to Get Through Those Long, Long High Holy Days Services

Count the number of women in mink coats.

✡

Now, the number of women in sable coats.

Identify whose stomach is rumbling
in the seat behind you—
without turning around!

Find the cutest person
of the opposite sex.

Begin sending that person telepathic
messages to bump into you out
on the steps afterward.

Time to put on more lip balm?

✡

Give yourself a "fingertip face lift."

✡

Baby crying in the child-care nursery:
yours?

Try to remember whether you turned the stove off before you left home.

Prepare a mental inventory of every item in your apartment, in case you did leave the stove on.

Think about what you'll wear tomorrow . . .

. . . And what you'll eat.

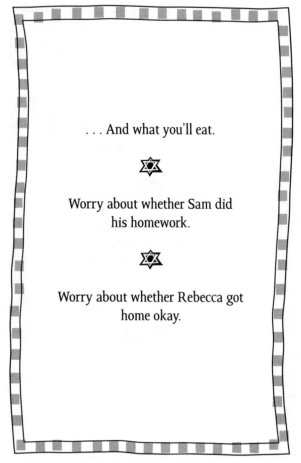

Worry about whether Sam did
his homework.

Worry about whether Rebecca got
home okay.

Worry about whether you have enough gasoline to drive home.

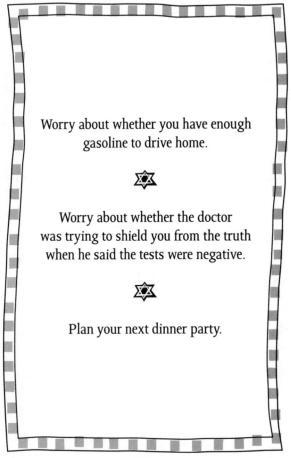

Worry about whether the doctor was trying to shield you from the truth when he said the tests were negative.

✡

Plan your next dinner party.

Try to open the hymnbook to
exactly page 253.

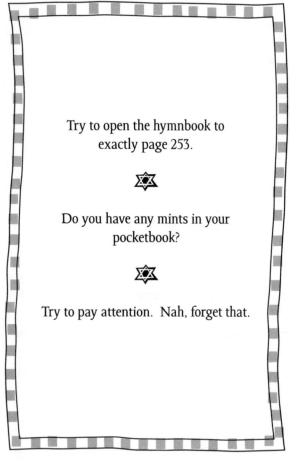

Do you have any mints in your
pocketbook?

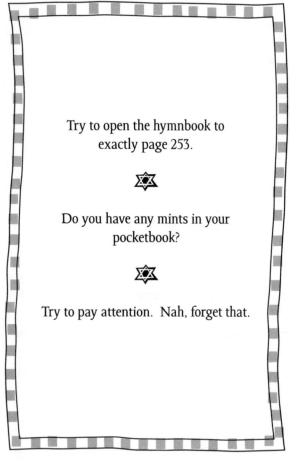

Try to pay attention.  Nah, forget that.

The High Holy Days are always an
excuse for a new suit or dress.

Or if you're very religious, a new hat.

Unlike Ramadan, Yom Kippur only
requires twenty-four hours' fasting.

The number 18 in
Hebrew signifies "life."

Leo Rosten's *The Joys of Yiddish*
is another kind of bible.

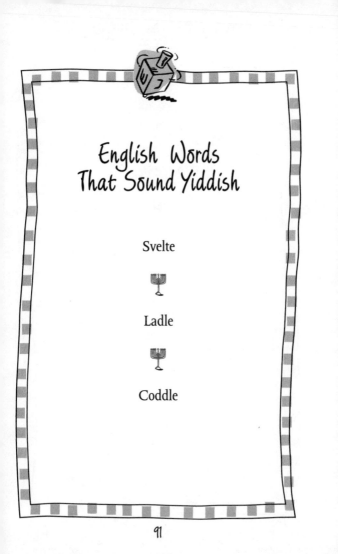

# English Words
# That Sound Yiddish

Svelte

Ladle

Coddle

Muddle

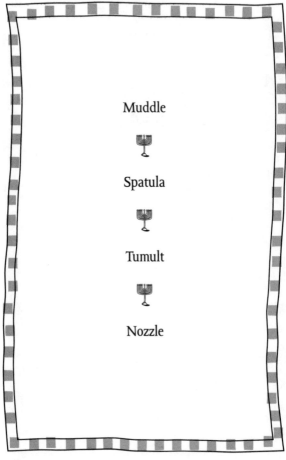

Spatula

Tumult

Nozzle

Phlegm

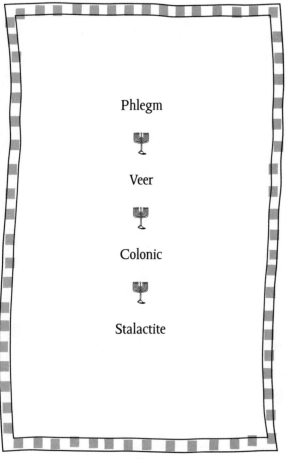

Veer

Colonic

Stalactite

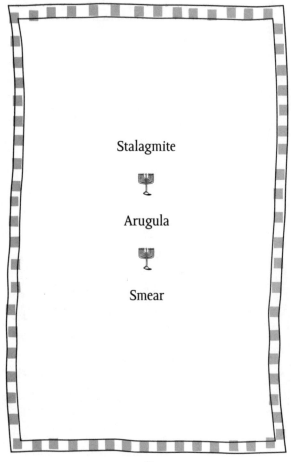

Stalagmite

Arugula

Smear

Our country clubs serve
unusually good food.

✡

Plenty of Biblical prophets to name
your kids after. (Your sons, at least.)

✡

Our coming-of-age ceremonies do not
involve ritual scarification.

That Maimonides—what a philosopher!

Gerda Lerner, an Austrian refugee who escaped
from the Nazis, is credited with creating the
field of women's studies.

"Let me tell you the one thing I have against
Moses. He took us forty years into the desert in
order to bring us to the one place in the Middle
East that has no oil!" —Golda Meir

# What Passersby Said About the Burning Bush

"Quick! Get the marshmallows!"

"Isn't it against zoning regulations to have a barbecue?"

"I hope we get some rain soon."

"Hmph! Real subtle."

"Ignore it; it's only trying to get attention."

"Surely there's a simpler way of getting His message across."

"Is it me or is it hot?"

"First the Levins' barn burns down.
Now this. What's next? The rain forest?"

"There goes the neighborhood."

"Man was not brought into the world to enjoy
himself." —Abraham ibn Ezra

You've got to give them credit for figuring out how
to get a sound out of a ram's horn.

Making an *aliya*.
Well, it's one way of leaving home.

"Dayanu" is so catchy that to hear it once is
to have it in your head for a week (alas).

You're *supposed* to make noise during the
reading of the megillah at Purim.

In Jewish tradition, wine is a symbol of joy.

In an observant household, there should also
be a mezuzah on the garage door.

(But you don't have to put any on the
closet or bathroom doors.)

# Little-Known Jewish Holidays

Rush-A-Shoppa: Observance of
the miracle of the 70 percent off sale.

Yummy Kippers: Celebration of
the Smoked Fishes.

T'ush A Vast: Day of atonement
for eating so many greasy foods.

Leftover:  Remembrance of the Foodstuff
in the Refrigerator.

Shame'outh:  Day on which you better
call your mother or else.

Passover and Over:  Week in which we
commemorate that time we got so lost
going to Aunt Myrna's.

Saccoth: Festival of Nice Luggage.

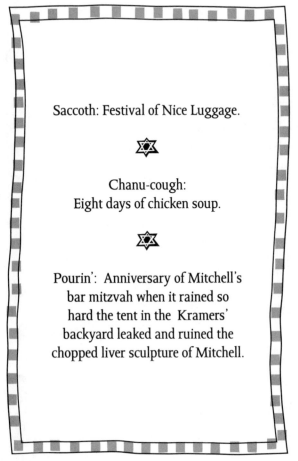

Chanu-cough:
Eight days of chicken soup.

Pourin': Anniversary of Mitchell's
bar mitzvah when it rained so
hard the tent in the Kramers'
backyard leaked and ruined the
chopped liver sculpture of Mitchell.

There are Hebrew fonts that can
be downloaded from AOL . . .

. . . And did you know you can get
Torah software for children?

No vowels in Hebrew.  Who needs them?

✡

Traditional Jews give at least 10 percent
of their income to charity.

Traditional Jewish homes have a *pushke*,
a box for collecting coins for the poor.

Suki met a great guy on J-date . . .
and they're getting married!

Monotheism?  Our idea.

Some of the nicest assisted living homes
are run by Jewish organizations.

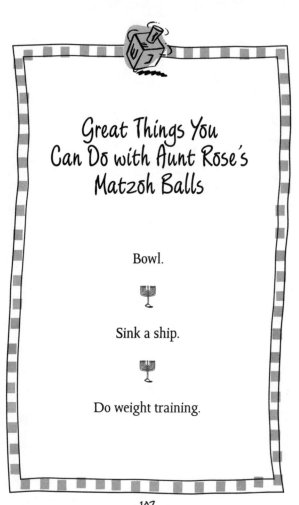

# Great Things You Can Do with Aunt Rose's Matzoh Balls

Bowl.

Sink a ship.

Do weight training.

Use as a paperweight . . .

. . . Or a knife sharpener . . .

. . . Or a doorstop.

Feed to the dog, and if the dog
turns them down . . .

. . . Feed to Uncle Irv.

Bury them.

We pretty much invented psychoanalysis . . .

. . . And kept it in business.

Though Yom Kippur tickets are expensive, you hardly ever see scalpers outside the synagogue.

Bribery will not get you into
God's Book of Life.

Susan Brownmiller's article "Sisterhood Is Powerful"—published in the *New York Times Sunday Magazine* in 1970—played a pivotal role in introducing the women's liberation movement to the American public.

On an airplane, ask for the kosher meal. Much better than what everyone else gets.

# Giveaway Lines That the Person in the Kosher Restaurant Is Not Jewish

"Waiter, my Dr. Brown's Cel-Ray soda has no celery in it."

✡

"Could you ask the piano player if he knows 'Amazing Grace'?"

✡

"I'll have the bacon cheeseburger."

"Is 'pareve' some sort of pasta?"

"Where's the butter dish?"

"This is better than the borscht at the convent."

"A malt beer, please."

You can plead ignorance and not fast
on Tishah-b'Ab.

The Israeli Day Parade is a good place
to pick up guys and gals.

Practically everyone speaks English in Israel.

✡

Feel free to skip many pages in the Haggadah.

A tallith can be a source of warmth on a cold day.

The Sheva Brachos are cheaper
than a honeymoon.

Some Jewish people watch TV not for
entertainment, but to call out the names of
Jewish actors and actresses.

# Original Names of Jewish Celebrities

Tony Randall:
Leonard Rosenberg

Tony Curtis:
Bernie Schwartz

Edward G. Robinson:
Emanuel Goldenberg

Dinah Shore:
Frances "Fanny" Rose Shore

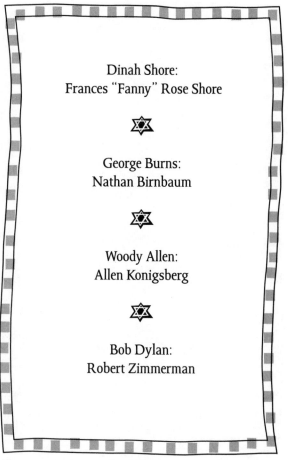

George Burns:
Nathan Birnbaum

Woody Allen:
Allen Konigsberg

Bob Dylan:
Robert Zimmerman

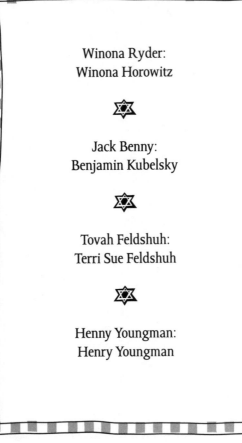

Winona Ryder:
Winona Horowitz

✡

Jack Benny:
Benjamin Kubelsky

✡

Tovah Feldshuh:
Terri Sue Feldshuh

✡

Henny Youngman:
Henry Youngman

Jon Stewart:
Jonathan Stuart Leibowitz

✡

Jane Seymour:
Joyce Frankenberg

✡

Jerry Lewis:
Joseph Levitch

✡

Shelly Winters:
Shirley Schrift

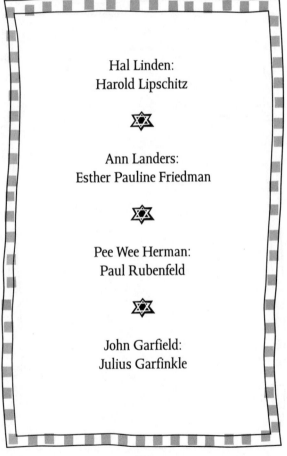

Hal Linden:
Harold Lipschitz

✡

Ann Landers:
Esther Pauline Friedman

✡

Pee Wee Herman:
Paul Rubenfeld

✡

John Garfield:
Julius Garfinkle

Lauren Bacall:
Betty Joan Perske

Rona Barrett:
Rona Burstein

Milton Berle:
Milton Berlinger

Irving Berlin:
Israel Baline

Andrew Dice Clay:
Andrew Silverstein

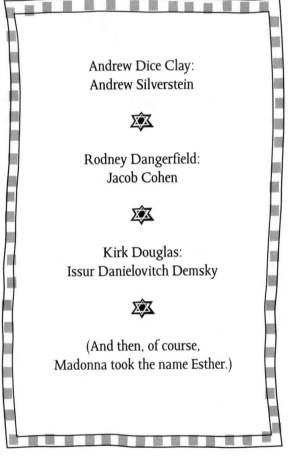

Rodney Dangerfield:
Jacob Cohen

Kirk Douglas:
Issur Danielovitch Demsky

(And then, of course,
Madonna took the name Esther.)

We believe in free will . . .

. . . Except when our children won't
practice their piano lessons.

We do not believe in original sin . . .

. . . Except sometimes when we think
about our exes.

The Ivy Leagues don't discriminate
against us any longer.

How 'bout that Betty Friedan?

Ruth Bader Ginsberg, the first Jewish
woman to serve on the U.S. Supreme Court,
has played an important role in assuring
equal treatment of women by defining sex
discrimination as a violation of the Constitution.

A large Jewish community in Tulsa, Oklahoma?
Yes.

✡

In Savannah, Georgia, too.

✡

There is a Jewish museum in Stockholm, Sweden.

✡

You have your name and your Jewish name *and*
your pre-Ellis-Island name.

# Milestones at the 92nd Street YMHA

In 1874, the Young Men's Hebrew
Association was founded by German
Jewish professionals and businessmen.
Dr. Simeon Newton Leo hosted
the first meeting at his home.
Rented quarters included parlors,
a reading room, and a gymnasium
acquired at 112 West 21st Street.

The Hebrew Free School for
boys and girls was started in 1907.

The new YMHA opened at 92nd Street and Lexington Avenue in 1900. The first High Holy Days services were held in 1900—a tradition that continues to the present day.

✡

Emma Lazarus taught immigrants at the 92nd Street Y well before she composed the famous poem for the base of the Statue of Liberty, "The New Colossus" ("Send us your tired, your poor, your huddled masses . . .").

In 1913, Boy Scout Troop 635 at the YMHA became the first troop organized by a Jewish community center in America.

The pioneers of modern dance—Martha Graham, Louis Horst, Hanya Holm, Charles Weidman, and Doris Humphrey—first presented their works there in the first-of-its-kind "Symposium on Modern Dance" in 1935. Agnes de Mille later said that without the 92nd Street Y, "the entire revolution in dance might not have succeeded."

In 1939, William Carlos Williams opened the first season of the Y's Unterberg Poetry Center.

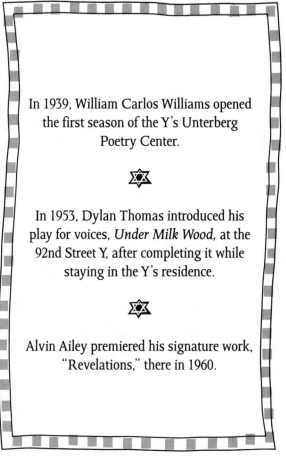

In 1953, Dylan Thomas introduced his play for voices, *Under Milk Wood*, at the 92nd Street Y, after completing it while staying in the Y's residence.

In 1960, Alvin Ailey premiered his signature work, "Revelations," there in 1960.

Elie Wiesel presented the first *Fascination with Jewish Tales* program in 1967.

✡

Cellist Yo-Yo Ma made his New York recital debut there in 1974.

✡

Camp Tova was established as the first day camp for children with special needs in 1982.

The Y housed newly arrived Russian Jewish immigrants in 1989.

The 92nd Street Y has the only pool in New York disinfected primarily with ozone. Unlike chlorine, ozone prevents bathing suits from fading, skin from drying, eyes from stinging, and pool water from having a pungent smell.

Guest speakers have included Bill Gates,
Mikhail Gorbachev, Gloria Steinem,
Jimmy Carter, and Kofi Annan.

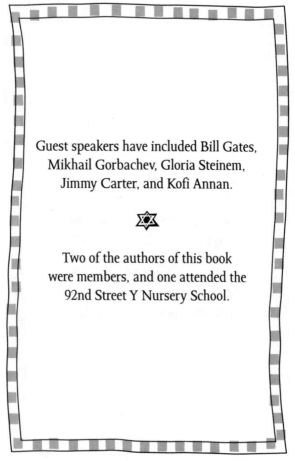

Two of the authors of this book
were members, and one attended the
92nd Street Y Nursery School.

"Let my people go!"  Wasn't that brave of Moses?

(Especially for someone who started
life in a basket.)

*Seinfeld* is really *ours*.

So is *Curb Your Enthusiasm*.

Wallabee shoes just kind of look . . . Jewish.

Q: What did the waiter
ask the group of Jewish mothers?
A: "Is anything okay?"

That Eeyore—what a kvetch!

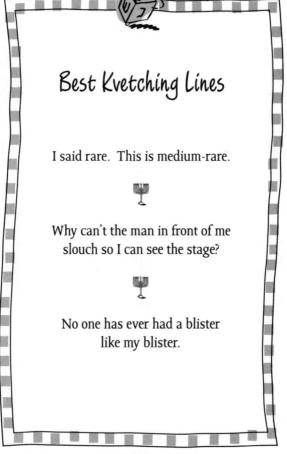

# Best Kvetching Lines

I said rare. This is medium-rare.

Why can't the man in front of me
slouch so I can see the stage?

No one has ever had a blister
like my blister.

The worst part? We got in for free,
so we couldn't get a refund.

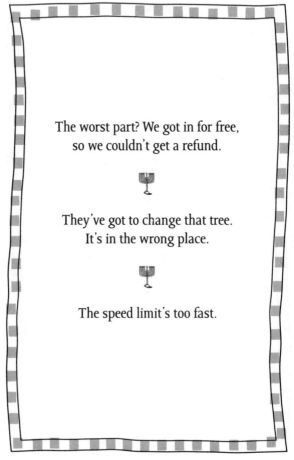

They've got to change that tree.
It's in the wrong place.

The speed limit's too fast.

This water has no taste.

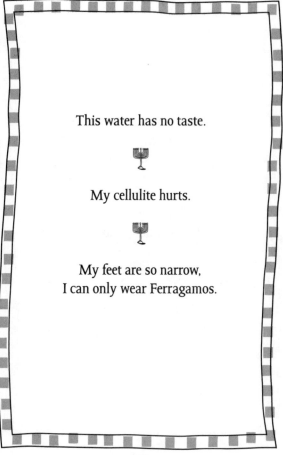

My cellulite hurts.

My feet are so narrow,
I can only wear Ferragamos.

This traffic is so bad you could
make a stuffed derma between
here and the next exit.

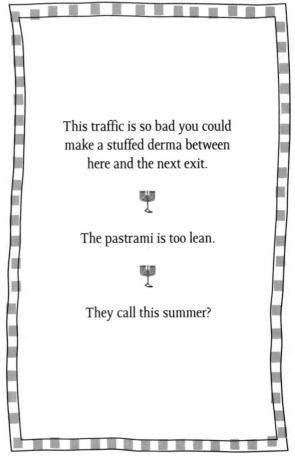

The pastrami is too lean.

They call this summer?

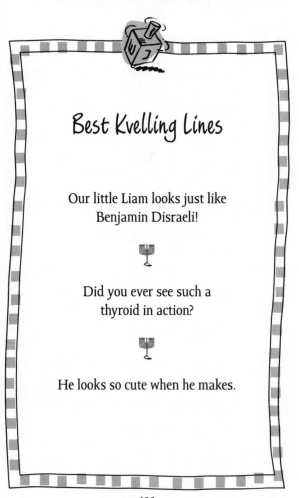

# Best Kvelling Lines

Our little Liam looks just like
Benjamin Disraeli!

Did you ever see such a
thyroid in action?

He looks so cute when he makes.

He scored a perfect Apgar!

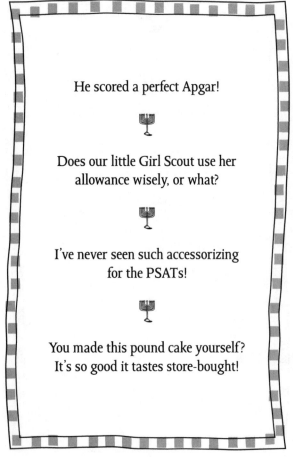

Does our little Girl Scout use her allowance wisely, or what?

I've never seen such accessorizing for the PSATs!

You made this pound cake yourself? It's so good it tastes store-bought!

Sophie Tucker had nothing
on our *shayna madele*.

Olivia got into Yale early decision.

I shouldn't tell you this, but the *mohel*
said he'd never seen anything that big.

You're going to think I'm bragging, but . . .

She does a perfect cartwheel. Watch!

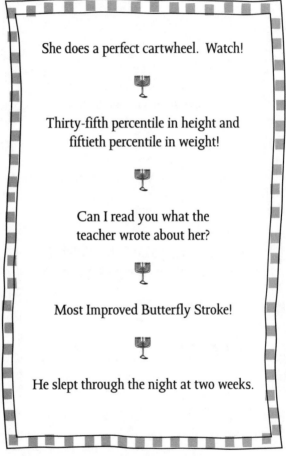

Thirty-fifth percentile in height and
fiftieth percentile in weight!

Can I read you what the
teacher wrote about her?

Most Improved Butterfly Stroke!

He slept through the night at two weeks.

You don't have to be Jewish to know
about the High Holy Days.

✡

You can always get inspired decorating
ideas from a *succah*.

✡

No such thing as a quickie rabbinic ordination,
so your Jewish wedding will be *legal*.

Kreplach are better than tortellini.

Kreplach is also the plural of kreplach.

Popes and cardinals also wear yarmulkes.

According to Billy Crystal, Yiddish is
a combination of German and phlegm.

# The Greatest Yiddish Words and Expressions

*A broch tzu Columbus!*—
A curse on Columbus!

*A chazzer bleibt a chazzer*—
A pig remains a pig.

*Az di bobe volt gehat beytsim*
*volt zi geven mayn zeyde!*—
If my grandmother had testicles,
she would be my grandfather!

*Bubeleh*—Sweetie, darling.

*Bulvan*—Oaf, brute.

*Bupkes*—Something totally worthless
(literally, beans).

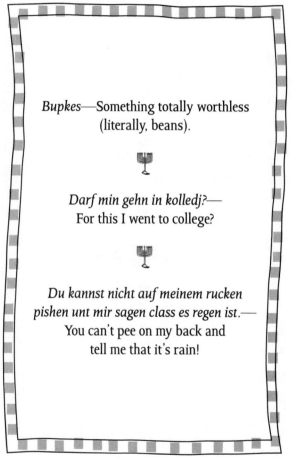

*Darf min gehn in kolledj?*—
For this I went to college?

*Du kannst nicht auf meinem rucken
pishen unt mir sagen class es regen ist.*—
You can't pee on my back and
tell me that it's rain!

*Ech hob in der drerd!*—Go to hell!

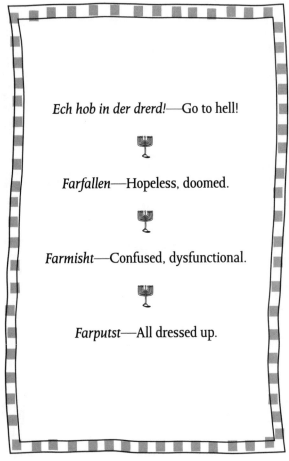

*Farfallen*—Hopeless, doomed.

*Farmisht*—Confused, dysfunctional.

*Farputst*—All dressed up.

*Farshluginer*—A bedraggled person.

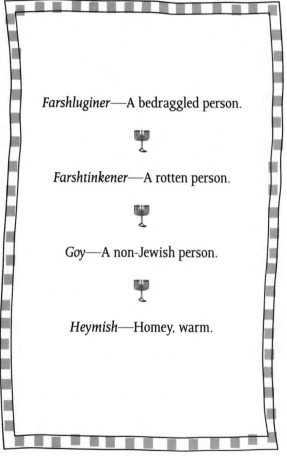

*Farshtinkener*—A rotten person.

*Goy*—A non-Jewish person.

*Heymish*—Homey, warm.

*Kibitzer*—Someone who's always joking.

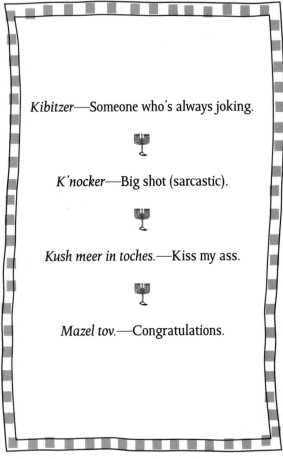

*K'nocker*—Big shot (sarcastic).

*Kush meer in toches.*—Kiss my ass.

*Mazel tov.*—Congratulations.

*Mensch*—Decent guy.

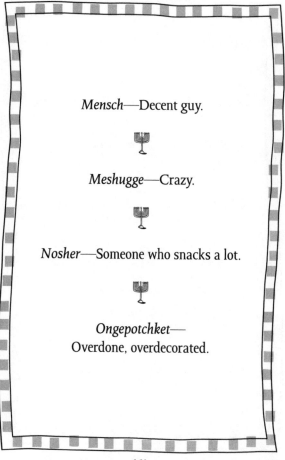

*Meshugge*—Crazy.

*Nosher*—Someone who snacks a lot.

*Ongepotchket*—
Overdone, overdecorated.

*Oygeshpilt*—Completely exhausted.

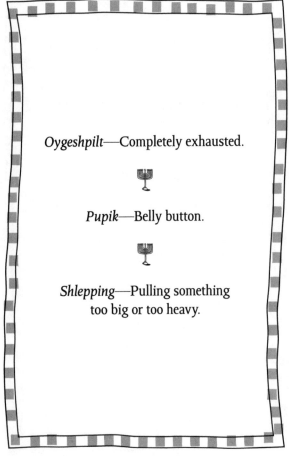

*Pupik*—Belly button.

*Shlepping*—Pulling something
too big or too heavy.

*Shlump*—A person wearing
his shirt untucked.

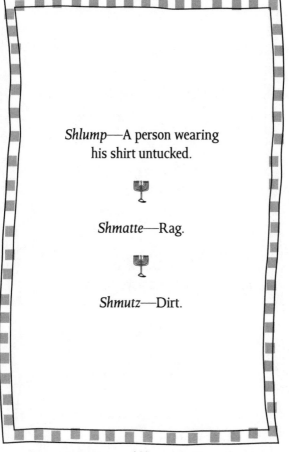

*Shmatte*—Rag.

*Shmutz*—Dirt.

*Shalom aleichem.*—
Hello, peace be with you.

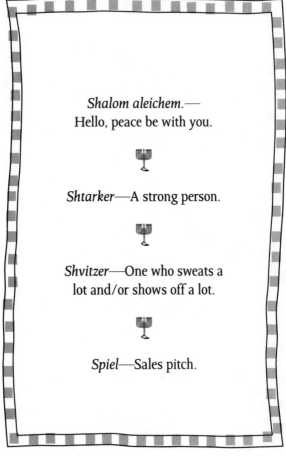

*Shtarker*—A strong person.

*Shvitzer*—One who sweats a
lot and/or shows off a lot.

*Spiel*—Sales pitch.

*Temper kop*—Dullard.

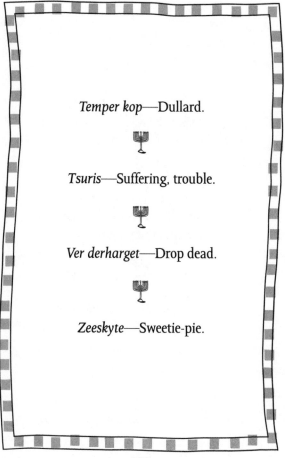

*Tsuris*—Suffering, trouble.

*Ver derharget*—Drop dead.

*Zeeskyte*—Sweetie-pie.

Barbie doesn't *seem* Jewish,
but no one said she wasn't Jewish, either.

Jews don't usually suffer from
bacterial-based diseases that come from
pork or pork by-products.

Even our tummies are sensitive!

We accept converts.

Yet we are not particularly proselytizers.

We are now comfortably ensconced in both
Palm Beach, Florida, and Greenwich, Connecticut.

Only in America do Isadore and Sadie
have grandchildren named Riley and Taylor.

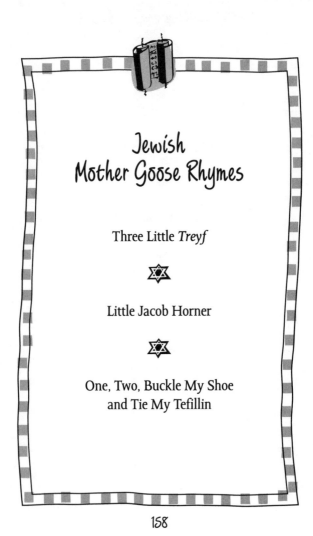

# Jewish
# Mother Goose Rhymes

Three Little *Treyf*

✡

Little Jacob Horner

✡

One, Two, Buckle My Shoe
and Tie My Tefillin

Pat a Sponge Cake, Pat a Sponge Cake

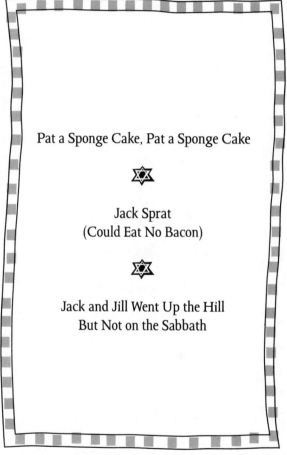

Jack Sprat
(Could Eat No Bacon)

Jack and Jill Went Up the Hill
But Not on the Sabbath

London Bridge Is Falling Down, Oy

✡

Miriam Had a Little Lamb

✡

Hot Cross Bagels

Twinkle, Twinkle, Little Star of David

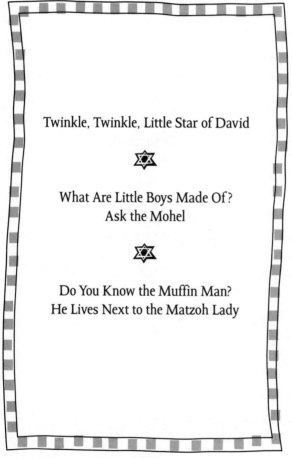

What Are Little Boys Made Of?
Ask the Mohel

Do You Know the Muffin Man?
He Lives Next to the Matzoh Lady

You can get into every movie
on Christmas day.

✡

And all the good Chinese
restaurants are open, too.

✡

"White Christmas" was written
by the Jewish Irving Berlin.

Lots of people wish they
had naturally curly hair.

✡

Many famous Motown R&B hits were
written by middle-aged Jewish men.

✡

So many sportscasters!

# Christianity Made Clear

You don't have to buy tickets for
important Christian church services.
They get you with the collection plate.

In real life, Jesus and Mary did not
have halos over their heads.

The Communion service has its origins
in the seder—not in cannibalism, the way
the Romans thought.

Protestants don't believe that the bread and wine at the Communion service are actually Christ's body and blood, but Catholics do.

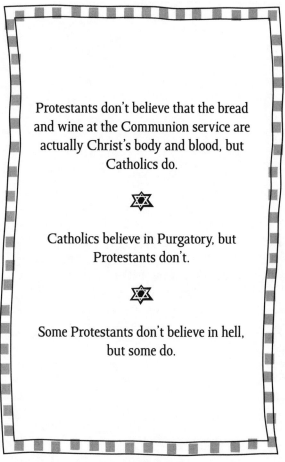

Catholics believe in Purgatory, but Protestants don't.

Some Protestants don't believe in hell, but some do.

Some of the people who speak in
tongues are faking it.

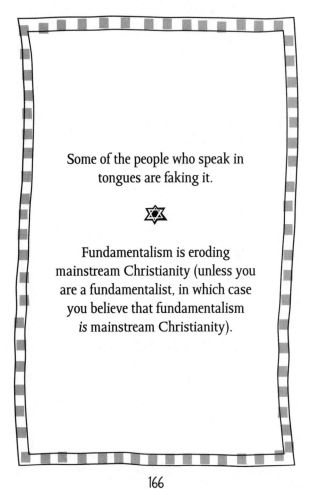

Fundamentalism is eroding
mainstream Christianity (unless you
are a fundamentalist, in which case
you believe that fundamentalism
*is* mainstream Christianity).

It's important not to leave Easter candy
where the dog can find it, because it
might make him sick.

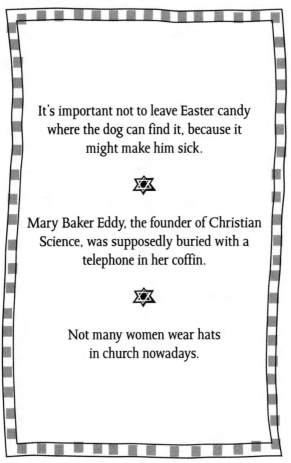

Mary Baker Eddy, the founder of Christian
Science, was supposedly buried with a
telephone in her coffin.

Not many women wear hats
in church nowadays.

Never trust a pastor who owns
a TV network.

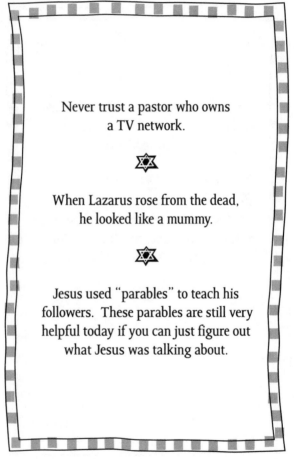

When Lazarus rose from the dead,
he looked like a mummy.

✡

Jesus used "parables" to teach his
followers. These parables are still very
helpful today if you can just figure out
what Jesus was talking about.

It's not true that Episcopalians reserve
the ninth circle of hell for people who
eat roast beef with their salad fork.

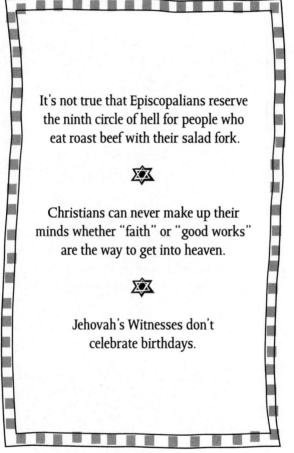

Christians can never make up their
minds whether "faith" or "good works"
are the way to get into heaven.

Jehovah's Witnesses don't
celebrate birthdays.

Mormons believe that Christ came
to North America and converted some
of the Native Americans.

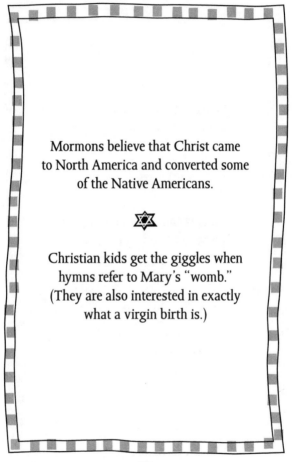

Christian kids get the giggles when
hymns refer to Mary's "womb."
(They are also interested in exactly
what a virgin birth is.)

The majority of Christmas-celebrating households use artificial Christmas trees.

✡

Jesus told us to turn the other cheek, but that didn't count for the Crusades.

✡

Mormons also call non-Mormons "gentiles."

It's not decreed in the Talmud, but when
a Jewish woman gives birth, her husband
usually buys her a lovely piece of jewelry.

✡

Tu B'Shevat: a holiday that celebrates
the birthday of the trees.

✡

An unspoken preference for good
silver serving pieces.

We have great summer sleepaway camps.

And these camps tend to have
Native American names.

And some of them have laundry services!

You'll never go hungry visiting us!

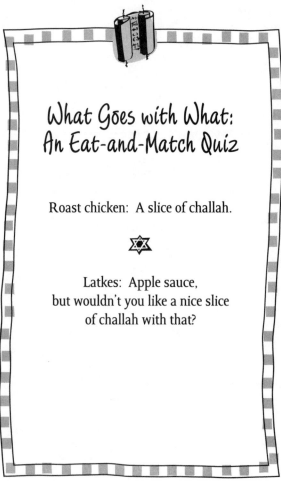

# What Goes with What: An Eat-and-Match Quiz

Roast chicken: A slice of challah.

✡

Latkes: Apple sauce,
but wouldn't you like a nice slice
of challah with that?

Matzoh ball soup:  A slice of challah.

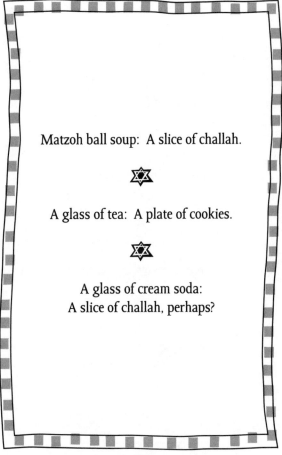

A glass of tea:  A plate of cookies.

A glass of cream soda:
A slice of challah, perhaps?

*Let's Make a Deal*'s Monty Hall is also a
cantor in Los Angeles.

We might not be the best athletes,
but we are great sports fans.

We never forget our mothers on Mother's Day.

Those Lactaid pills make it much easier
to be lactose-intolerant.

You always have a cousin or friend in the diamond business.

Did we mention that there is no hell in Judaism?

Women and men can equally serve as rabbis and cantors.

And they can get married and everything.

No one will make you convert, but if
you wanted to, you would be welcomed.

✡

Many Buddhists are also Jewish.

✡

It's probably easier to study Kabbalah
if you know Hebrew.

# Key Differences Between Judaism and Kabbalism

One spelling (Judaism) *vs* many spellings (Kabbalah, Qabalah, Cabala, Qaballah, Qabala, Kaballah, whatever).

Jewish women wear diamond jewelry; Kabbalists wear red string.

Torah *vs* Zohar.

Jewish people are happy to drink
Perrier with lime; Kabbalists are supposed
to buy special bottled Kabbalah water.

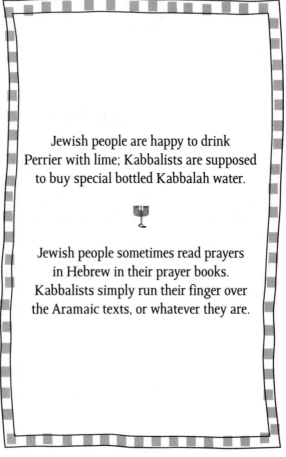

Jewish people sometimes read prayers
in Hebrew in their prayer books.
Kabbalists simply run their finger over
the Aramaic texts, or whatever they are.

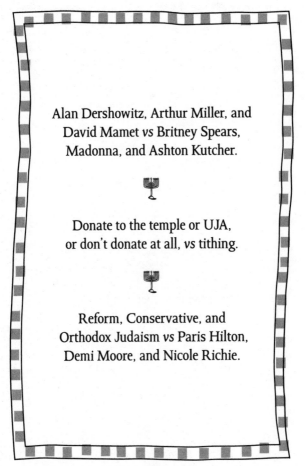

Alan Dershowitz, Arthur Miller, and
David Mamet vs Britney Spears,
Madonna, and Ashton Kutcher.

Donate to the temple or UJA,
or don't donate at all, vs tithing.

Reform, Conservative, and
Orthodox Judaism vs Paris Hilton,
Demi Moore, and Nicole Richie.

Amadeo Modigliani

We are the chosen people.

We know the difference between
Nova Scotia and lox.

Circumcisions promote good hygiene
and good health.

Josh, our youth leader, is really cute
and just graduated from Penn.

Brandeis University

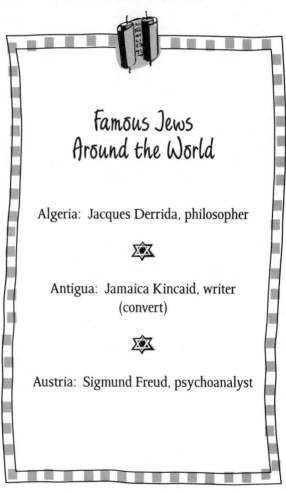

# Famous Jews
# Around the World

Algeria:  Jacques Derrida, philosopher

✡

Antigua:  Jamaica Kincaid, writer
(convert)

✡

Austria:  Sigmund Freud, psychoanalyst

Azerbaijan:  Garry Kasparov,
chess master

Belarus:  Marc Chagall, painter

Bulgaria:  Elias Canetti, Nobel Prize
winner for literature

Canada:  Leonard Cohen,
singer and poet

Czech Republic: Franz Kafka, writer

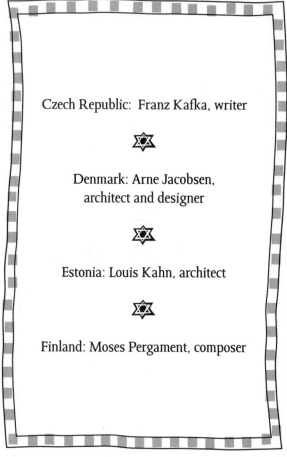

Denmark: Arne Jacobsen,
architect and designer

Estonia: Louis Kahn, architect

Finland: Moses Pergament, composer

France: Emile Durkheim, sociologist

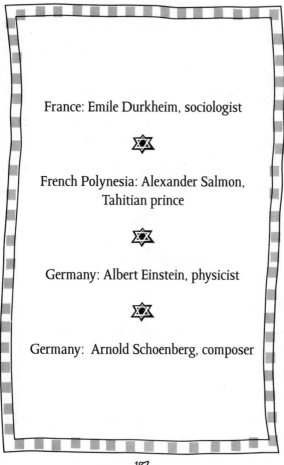

French Polynesia: Alexander Salmon,
Tahitian prince

Germany: Albert Einstein, physicist

Germany:  Arnold Schoenberg, composer

Greece: Hank Azaria, actor

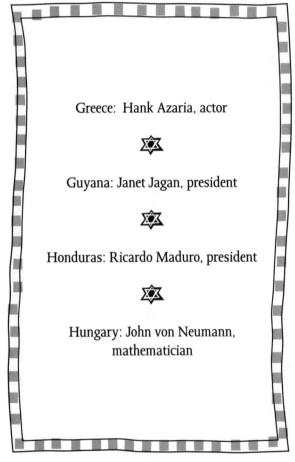

Guyana: Janet Jagan, president

Honduras: Ricardo Maduro, president

Hungary: John von Neumann,
mathematician

Iceland:  Dorrit Moussaieff, first lady

India: Nissim Ezekial, poet

India: Elie Tahari, designer

Iraq: Maurice and Charles Saatchi,
advertisers

Ireland: Chaim Herzog,
president of Israel

Israel: Itzhak Perlman, violinist

Latvia: Isaiah Berlin, philosopher

Lebanon: Edmund Safra, banker

Lithuania: Emma Goldman, anarchist

Mexico: Frieda Kahlo, painter
(Jewish father)

Myanmar: Ike Isaacs, jazz player

Netherlands: Baruch Spinoza,
philosopher

Panama: Eric Arturo Delvalle, president

Peru: Isaac Goldemberg, poet

✡

Poland: Roman Polanski, director

✡

Romania: Sami Rosenstock, poet

Russia: Boris Pasternak, poet

Slovakia: Ivan Reitman, director

South Africa: Nadine Gordimer, writer

Spain: Louis Vaez de Torres, explorer

Sweden: Oskar Klein, physicist

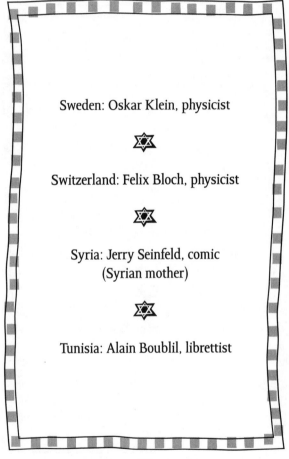

Switzerland: Felix Bloch, physicist

Syria: Jerry Seinfeld, comic
(Syrian mother)

Tunisia: Alain Boublil, librettist

Turkey: Neil Sedaka, singer/songwriter
(Turkish father)

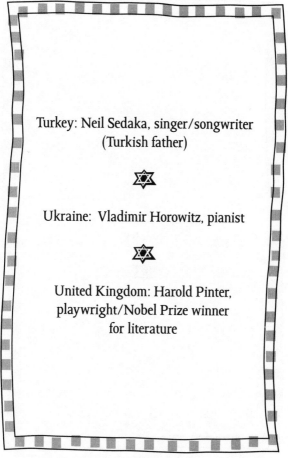

Ukraine: Vladimir Horowitz, pianist

United Kingdom: Harold Pinter,
playwright/Nobel Prize winner
for literature

United States: Bob Dylan,
singer/songwriter

Virgin Islands: Camille Pissarro,
painter

Zambia: Stanley Fischer, economist

What would *The Ed Sullivan Show*
have been without George Burns, Jack Benny,
Milton Berle, Henny Youngman, Buddy Hackett,
Alan King, Shelley Berman, Woody Allen,
Jackie Mason, Totie Fields, Joan Rivers,
David Brenner, or Jerry Stiller?

✡

And speaking of funny: Neil Simon, Mel Brooks,
Carl Reiner, to mention a few more.

Mort Sahl, Lenny Bruce, the Three Stooges,
Jerry Lewis, Andy Kaufman, Sandra Bernhart,
Gilda Radner . . . we can't resist.

Roseanne Barr, Jason Alexander, Adam Sandler.
We could go on, but we'll leave it at that.

## Attributes of Jewish Grandparents

Do not know the word "No."

🕎

Allow you to forage for treasures in
special drawers that were kept
off-limits to your parents
at the same age.

Serve meals all hours of day and night
in order to "fatten you up."

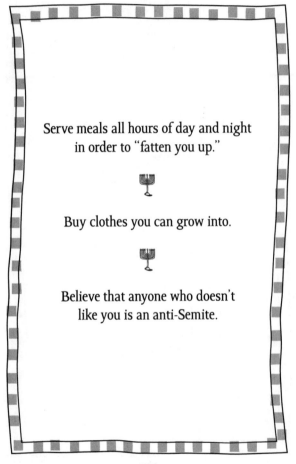

Buy clothes you can grow into.

Believe that anyone who doesn't
like you is an anti-Semite.

Tell all the other grandparents
in the complex about you and
your clarinet solo.

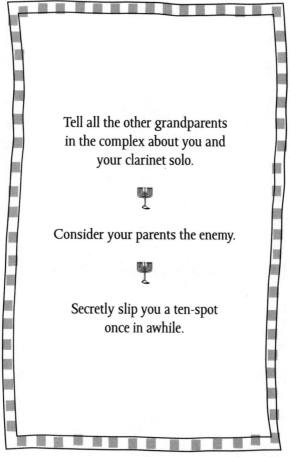

Consider your parents the enemy.

Secretly slip you a ten-spot
once in awhile.

Suddenly remember all those
Yiddish expressions they
heard as children.

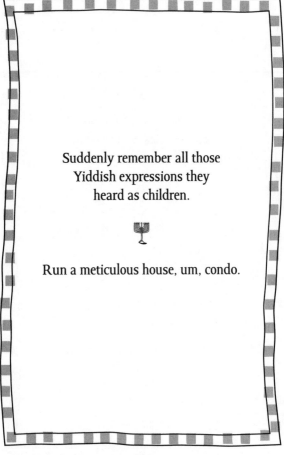

Run a meticulous house, um, condo.

Some of us *really* know how to shop.

Our men are said to make great husbands.

So many people are allergic to shellfish, anyway.

We don't have to worry about
the crab salad being rancid.

We tend not to be daredevils . . .

. . . Or even travel without our allergy medicines.

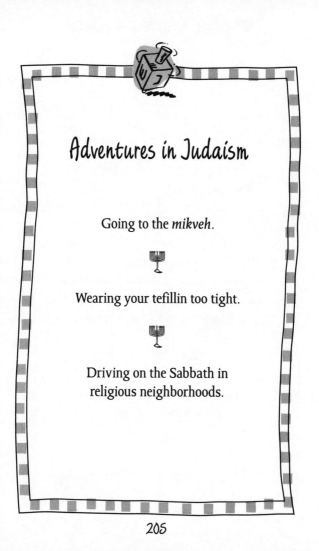

# Adventures in Judaism

Going to the *mikveh*.

Wearing your tefillin too tight.

Driving on the Sabbath in
religious neighborhoods.

Parking in front of a temple on a
Saturday—even worse if you're a Jew.

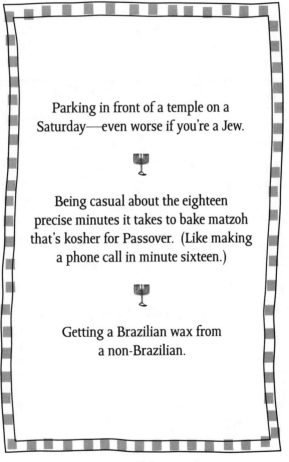

Being casual about the eighteen
precise minutes it takes to bake matzoh
that's kosher for Passover. (Like making
a phone call in minute sixteen.)

Getting a Brazilian wax from
a non-Brazilian.

Getting circumcised as an adult.

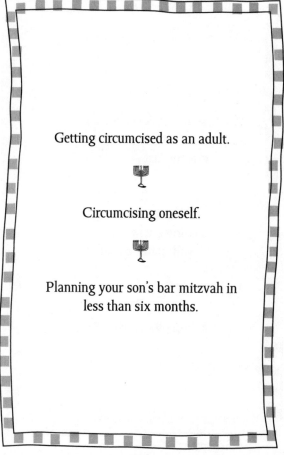

Circumcising oneself.

Planning your son's bar mitzvah in
less than six months.

Buying the dress you want to wear
at your son's bar mitzvah before you
lose the last six pounds.

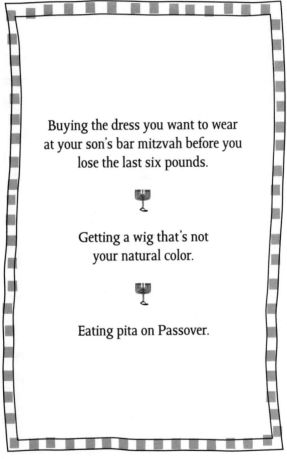

Getting a wig that's not
your natural color.

Eating pita on Passover.

Dating a boy you met at
Gina's church picnic.

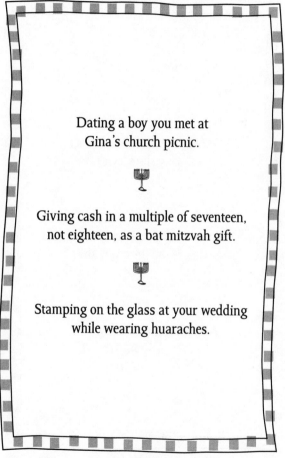

Giving cash in a multiple of seventeen,
not eighteen, as a bat mitzvah gift.

Stamping on the glass at your wedding
while wearing huaraches.

Taking out your Blackberry
during the service.

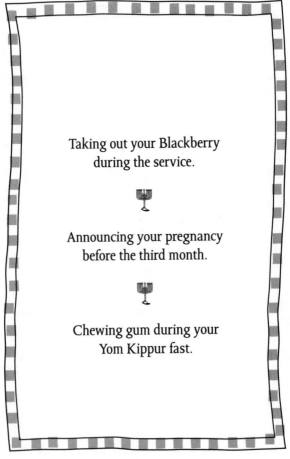

Announcing your pregnancy
before the third month.

Chewing gum during your
Yom Kippur fast.

Wearing your yarmulke inside out.

Making chicken soup
without chicken fat.

Taking part in a high-stakes
dreidel game.

Christmas caroling.

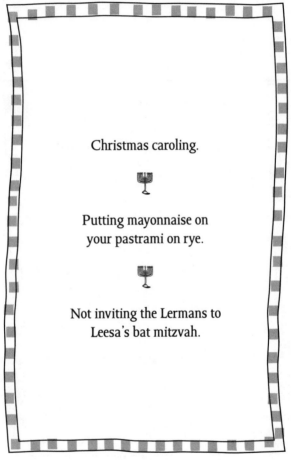

Putting mayonnaise on
your pastrami on rye.

Not inviting the Lermans to
Leesa's bat mitzvah.

Instead of going to confession every week,
we just go once a year, and try not to eat
for twenty-four hours.

Non-Jews seem to like our pastrami sandwiches.

And our pumpernickel.

We never serve skimpy portions.

Sandy Koufax

Jesus, of course, was one of us.

And Madonna studies the Kabbalah.

The Israelites, led by Moses, trekked through the desert for forty years on their journey to Israel: the original Outward Bound.

# Possible Locations of the Ten Lost Tribes of Israel

Still trying to find parking.

A beautiful condo in Miami Beach.

Waiting in line for tickets to the new Andrew Lloyd Webber musical.

Produce department, trying to
pick out a ripe melon.

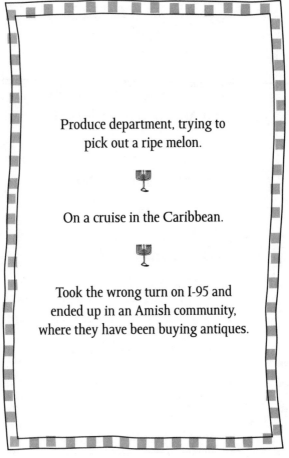

On a cruise in the Caribbean.

Took the wrong turn on I-95 and
ended up in an Amish community,
where they have been buying antiques.

Taking ballroom dancing lessons to be ready for the Meltzer bar mitzvah.

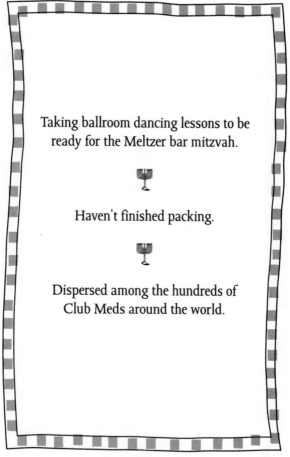

Haven't finished packing.

Dispersed among the hundreds of Club Meds around the world.

I know I saw them right over there . . .
just a few thousand years ago.

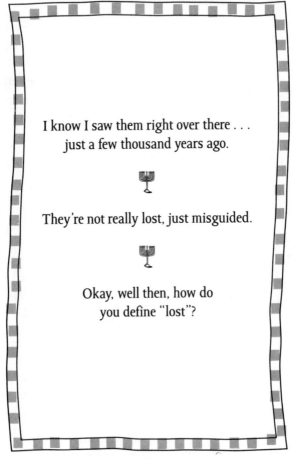

They're not really lost, just misguided.

Okay, well then, how do
you define "lost"?

The Lost Island of Atlantis.

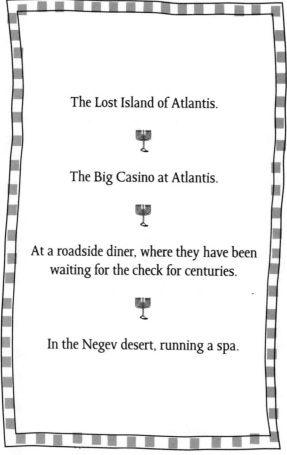

The Big Casino at Atlantis.

At a roadside diner, where they have been
waiting for the check for centuries.

In the Negev desert, running a spa.

Taking Wednesday morning adult swim classes at the JCC.

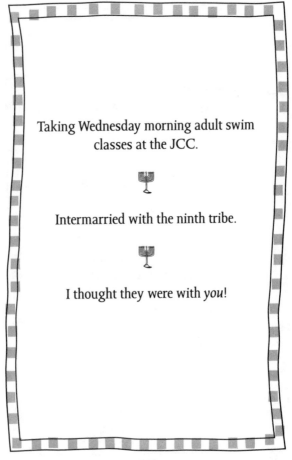

Intermarried with the ninth tribe.

I thought they were with *you!*

Live on a kibbutz, and you will never
have to find a babysitter again.

Most of those Ten Commandments still hold up.

Lighting the Sabbath candles is *almost*
as much fun for a child as pressing the
button on the elevator.

According to Genesis, Noah lived five
hundred years, so he must have been
doing something right.

The Yiddish Theater in New York put on
works by Ibsen, Tolstoy, and Shaw before those
playwrights were performed on Broadway.

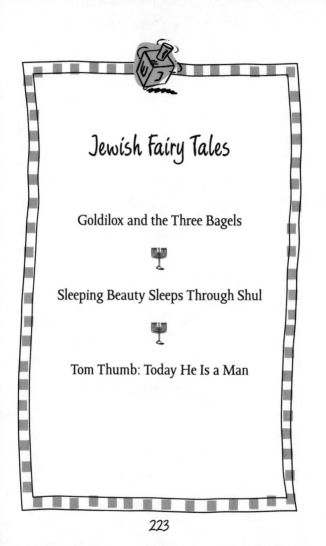

# Jewish Fairy Tales

Goldilox and the Three Bagels

Sleeping Beauty Sleeps Through Shul

Tom Thumb: Today He Is a Man

The Princess and the Pea . . .
That's All You're Eating?!

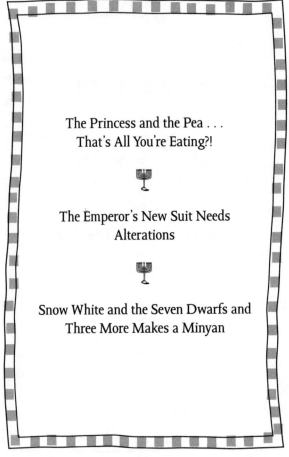

The Emperor's New Suit Needs
Alterations

Snow White and the Seven Dwarfs and
Three More Makes a Minyan

Hansel and Gretel Go to Medical School

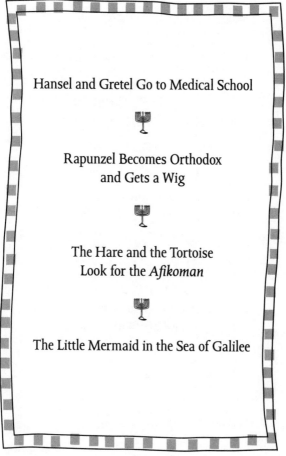

Rapunzel Becomes Orthodox
and Gets a Wig

The Hare and the Tortoise
Look for the *Afikoman*

The Little Mermaid in the Sea of Galilee

More likely than non-Jews to be
able to answer the Balfour Declaration
questions in Trivial Pursuit games.

Our ancestors probably did not come over
on the Mayflower . . . is that a good thing?

Did you know that our friend Russell's
great-great-great-great-grandfather was
chief rabbi of Lithuania?

What's better than a smart Jewish doctor?

You really shouldn't visit Venice without visiting the Jewish ghetto there—it's the oldest Jewish ghetto in the world.

"Don't be so humble—you are not that great."
—Golda Meir

# Other Uses for a Shofar

Back scratcher.

✡

Receptacle for hard candies.

✡

Ice-cream scoop.

Shoehorn.

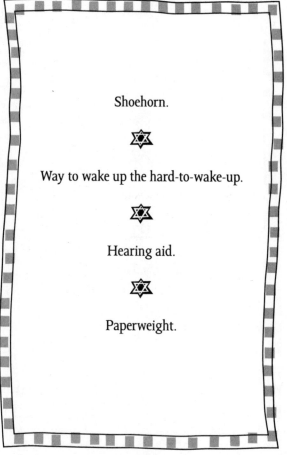

Way to wake up the hard-to-wake-up.

Hearing aid.

Paperweight.

Ivy planter.

Candle snuffer.

If you're not using it, the
ram might want it back.

The discovery of the Dead Sea Scrolls was almost as exciting as *Raiders of the Lost Ark*.

✡

The mystery of the Ten Lost Tribes of Israel is almost as intriguing as Agatha Christie's *And Then There Were None*.

✡

My, that United Jewish Appeal does good works.

Aunt Ruth stayed up all night
making *hamentaschen*.

Marc Chagall's stained glass windows
are just beautiful.

The Star of David: so easy to draw!

Orthodox Jews use less energy . . .
at least on Saturdays.

And speaking of energy conservation:
The Jews were so thrilled about a little oil
lasting longer than expected that they
invented Chanukah.

There are so many interpretations about
why a glass is broken during the Jewish
wedding ceremony that everyone can be right.

# Great Things About Jewish Weddings

More cash gets slipped into grooms' pockets.

✡

Lots and lots of attendants.

✡

Kosher lamb chops are the ultimate lamb chops.

234

The guy gets to step on the glass
and look incredibly macho.

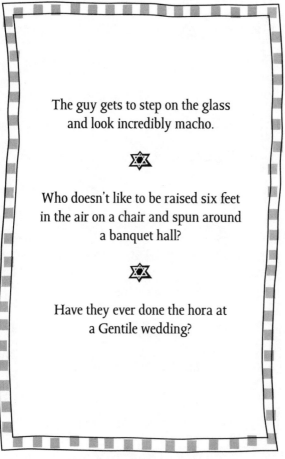

Who doesn't like to be raised six feet
in the air on a chair and spun around
a banquet hall?

Have they ever done the hora at
a Gentile wedding?

The bride's mother and father may both walk her down the aisle.

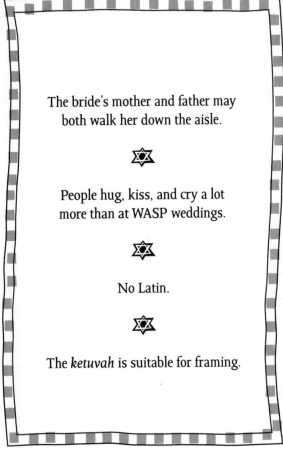

People hug, kiss, and cry a lot more than at WASP weddings.

No Latin.

The *ketuvah* is suitable for framing.

In a pinch, a handkerchief can
serve as a chuppah.

Sure is a lot of wine sipping
in the ceremony!

Dancing is a mitzvah.

We were pretty good boxers once upon a time.

Really, 2000+ seems such a puny
number compared to the almost six thousand
years on the Jewish calendar.

Go ahead. Tell your boss you're taking
the day off to observe . . . um,
Yom Davouth Hasashana.

Israel sure is in the news a lot.

What, us worry?

Chicken fat is better than it sounds.

(Okay, not much better.)

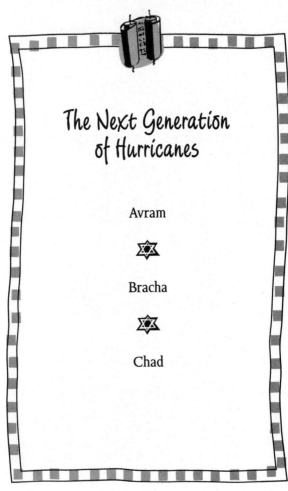

# The Next Generation of Hurricanes

Avram

✡

Bracha

✡

Chad

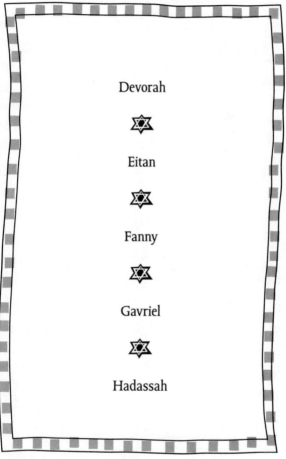

Devorah

✡

Eitan

✡

Fanny

✡

Gavriel

✡

Hadassah

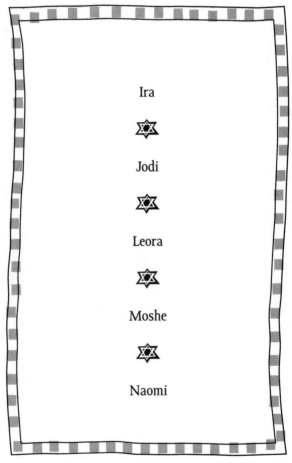

Ira

✡

Jodi

✡

Leora

✡

Moshe

✡

Naomi

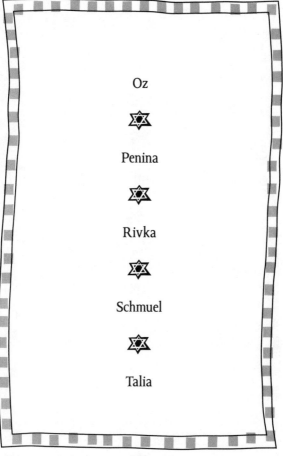

Oz

Penina

Rivka

Schmuel

Talia

Uriel

✡

Vardiya

✡

Yitzak

✡

Zehava

Jews don't have the answers; they'd rather keep asking questions.

The Torah, like a guitar, has its own case.

Plenty of food, and never a cash bar.

Thanks to the Diaspora,
Jews are spread all over the world.

The world owes us a big
thank-you for bagels.

Did we invent guilt?

Play your cards right, and you can haul
in a lot of loot for your bar or bat mitzvah.

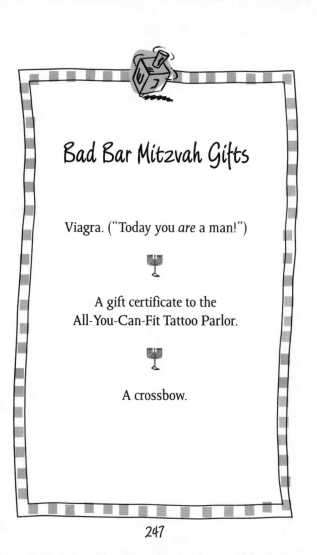

# Bad Bar Mitzvah Gifts

Viagra. ("Today you *are* a man!")

A gift certificate to the
All-You-Can-Fit Tattoo Parlor.

A crossbow.

A fake ID.

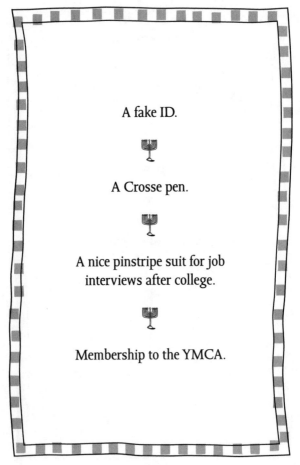

A Crosse pen.

A nice pinstripe suit for job
interviews after college.

Membership to the YMCA.

Christmas tree decorations.

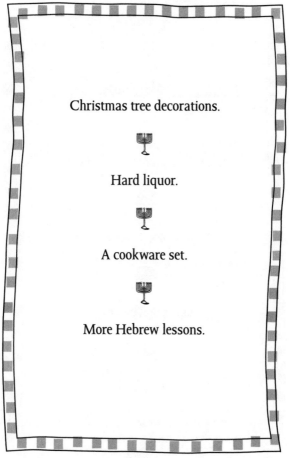

Hard liquor.

A cookware set.

More Hebrew lessons.

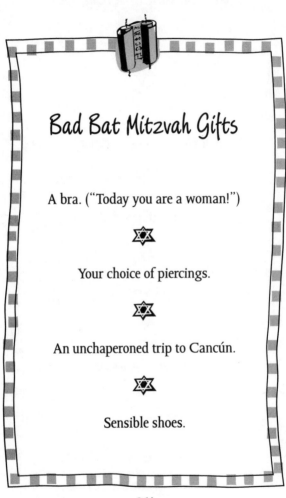

# Bad Bat Mitzvah Gifts

A bra. ("Today you are a woman!")

✡

Your choice of piercings.

✡

An unchaperoned trip to Cancún.

✡

Sensible shoes.

Aunt Linda's stupid garnet
brooch from the old days.

✡

A twenty-session gift certificate
to Weight Watchers.

✡

Chanel No.5 or similar old-lady perfume.

Vintage "Mystery Date" game bought
for an unspecified sum on eBay.

Support hose.

✡

One of those pot-holder-weaving looms.

✡

An E-Z Pass.

Getting cash at your wedding sure beats getting
another pair of crystal candlesticks.

Reform, Conservative, Orthodox: Pick your flavor.

A yarmulke hides bald spots.

Low rates of alcoholism. (How much
Mogen David can a person drink, after all?).

All that business we give Chinese
restaurants on Christmas Eve.

Is Passover before or after Easter this year?

Matchmaking wasn't such a bad idea.

If you go to a Jewish school, you *can't*
do homework on Saturdays.

If they're going to call you a "Jewish mother,"
you might as well be one.

✡

Being a "Jewish mother" is just another
way to say you care.

✡

Q: Define "genius."
A: A C-student with a Jewish mother.

You get big points for making your
latkes from scratch.

✡

School cafeterias have to serve matzoh during
Passover. It's practically a law.

✡

Unlike Catholics, you at least get to learn a new
language in your religious education classes.

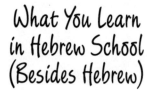

# What You Learn in Hebrew School (Besides Hebrew)

Going to after-school school makes for a *lot* of school.

♦

The snacks that Miriam's mom gives her are way better than the snacks your mom gives you.

But at least *your* mom picks
you up on time.

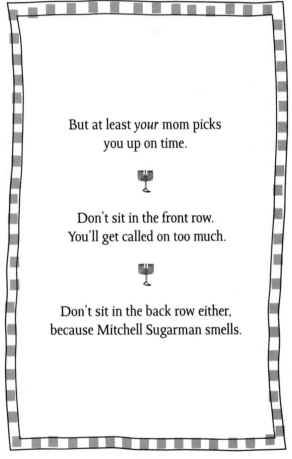

Don't sit in the front row.
You'll get called on too much.

Don't sit in the back row either,
because Mitchell Sugarman smells.

In the summer, you can sometimes
see into Mrs. Adler's shirts and
get a look at her bra.

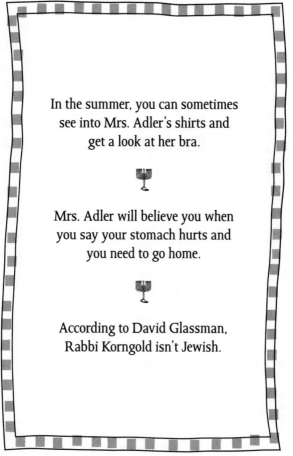

Mrs. Adler will believe you when
you say your stomach hurts and
you need to go home.

According to David Glassman,
Rabbi Korngold isn't Jewish.

If you let Bruce Silverman copy
off your paper, he'll give you some
really good baseball cards.

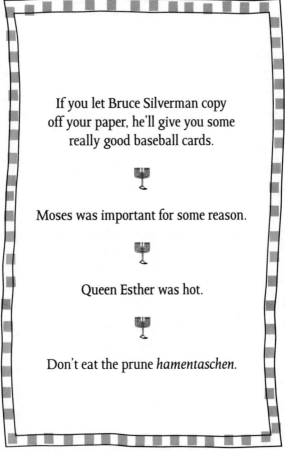

Moses was important for some reason.

Queen Esther was hot.

Don't eat the prune *hamentaschen*.

The Temple was destroyed, like, a million times.

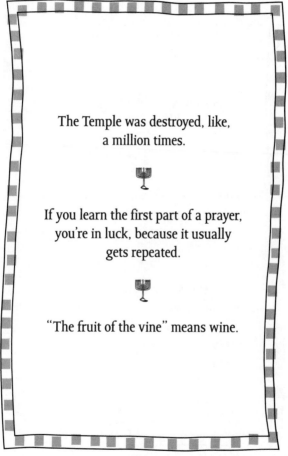

If you learn the first part of a prayer, you're in luck, because it usually gets repeated.

"The fruit of the vine" means wine.

Homework is bad, no matter
what language it's in.

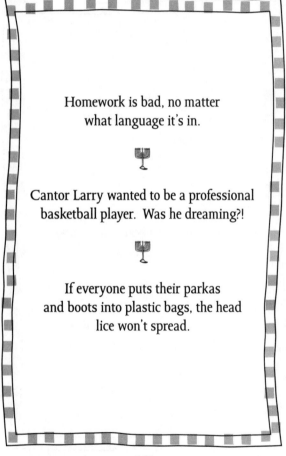

Cantor Larry wanted to be a professional
basketball player. Was he dreaming?!

If everyone puts their parkas
and boots into plastic bags, the head
lice won't spread.

By the time you're in seventh grade, you've made enough clay menorahs to last a lifetime.

The boys don't mind Israeli Folk Dancing as much as they pretend.

PowerPoint presentations about Hebrew traditions are just as boring as PowerPoint presentations about your dental health in regular school.

It is impossible to make a decent
dreidel out of papier-mâché.

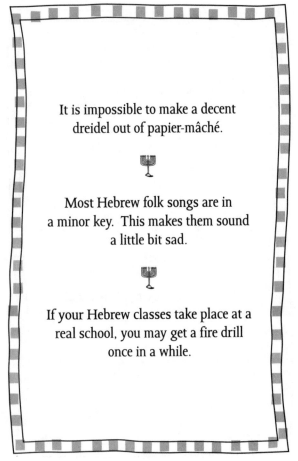

Most Hebrew folk songs are in
a minor key.  This makes them sound
a little bit sad.

If your Hebrew classes take place at a
real school, you may get a fire drill
once in a while.

Mrs. Adler's having problems
at home—you heard her talking
to one of the parents.

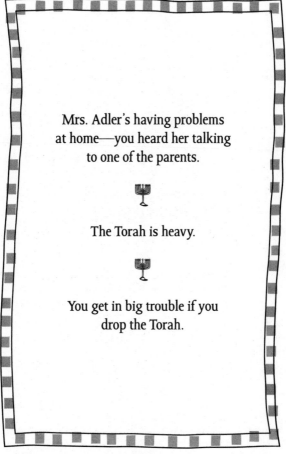

The Torah is heavy.

The Torah is heavy.

You get in big trouble if you
drop the Torah.

Yay! I finally got Gimmel!

You're not required to believe in the
Resurrection or the Virgin Birth.

Where else does a thirteen-year-old boy
get to say, "Today I am a man"?

*"Nes gadol haya sham."*
A great miracle happened there.

✡

No scratchy First Communion dresses required.

✡

Jewish parents encourage their kids
to take music lessons.

The only world religion with a Wailing Wall.

✡

You can get someone else to drive
you on the Sabbath.

✡

(And also turn your stove on and off.)

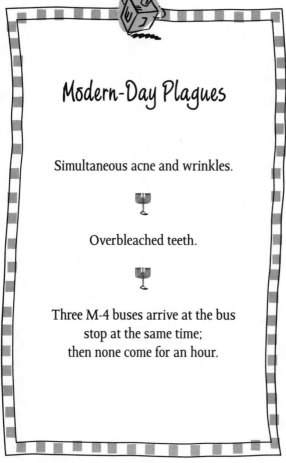

# Modern-Day Plagues

Simultaneous acne and wrinkles.

Overbleached teeth.

Three M-4 buses arrive at the bus
stop at the same time;
then none come for an hour.

Heavy, heavy backpacks.

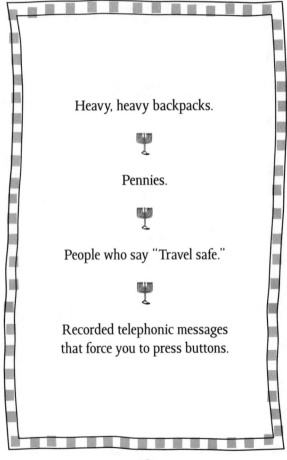

Pennies.

People who say "Travel safe."

Recorded telephonic messages
that force you to press buttons.

Plastic bags stuck in trees.

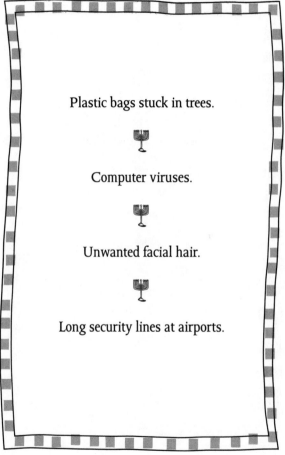

Computer viruses.

Unwanted facial hair.

Long security lines at airports.

Traffic on the
George Washington Bridge.

Ticketmaster surcharges.

Dozens of people smoking in the
cold outside office buildings, blocking
your entrance all winter long.

More than two women at one
time wearing Giorgio perfume
in the ladies' room.

Reality television.

The compulsion to get one's kids into
the best damn preschool in town.

The invasion of the Dance Motivators.

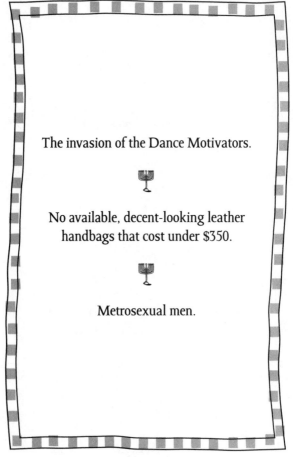

No available, decent-looking leather
handbags that cost under $350.

Metrosexual men.

The Diamond District.

Lighten up, they're playing klezmer.

Elizabeth Taylor converted when
she married Eddie Fisher.

So did Marilyn Monroe, when she
married Arthur Miller.

(So did Sammy Davis Jr.,
for some reason.)

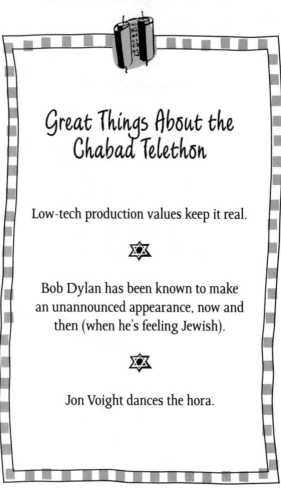

# Great Things About the Chabad Telethon

Low-tech production values keep it real.

✡

Bob Dylan has been known to make an unannounced appearance, now and then (when he's feeling Jewish).

✡

Jon Voight dances the hora.

Jon Voight used to dance the hora
with Jan Murray.

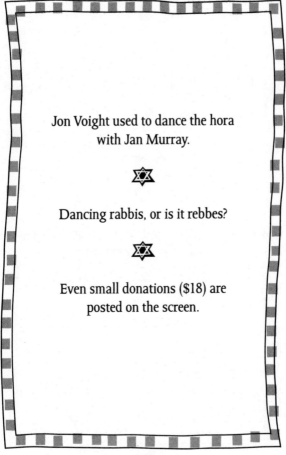

Dancing rabbis, or is it rebbes?

Even small donations ($18) are
posted on the screen.

The theme music for *Exodus* is so stirring.

*Haroseth* cancels out the bitter herbs.

Cool-looking blue-and-silver wrapping paper
instead of red and green.

The Marx Brothers.

They have great-looking menorahs
in the MoMA gift shop.

Fifteen percent of all Nobel laureates are Jewish.

"Sabbath is a day of peace between
man and nature." —Erich Fromm

Wow, King Solomon was wise.

# Unsung Heroes of the Bible

Mrs. Noah.

The guy who wove the bulrush basket
Moses was found in.

And the tailor who made the
coat of many colors.

And Joshua's trumpet-maker.

Sarah, for having a baby when she was a kajillion years old.

Isaac—for obvious reasons.

The lion in the den with Daniel.
He never asked for the fight.

✡

Naomi. Who says she *wanted*
Ruth following her around everywhere?

✡

The whale that swallowed Jonah and
probably suffered intense cramps for days.

The baby King Solomon suggested cutting in half to find out which woman was its true mother.

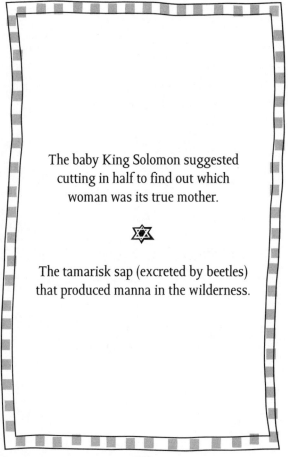

The tamarisk sap (excreted by beetles) that produced manna in the wilderness.

"A Jewish wife will forgive and forget, but she'll never forget what she forgave."

To Nana, everything you do is perfect.

"I have a little dreidel, I made it out of clay . . ."

*Sufganiyot* are way better than ordinary jelly doughnuts.

Bookbinders traditionally get a holiday on Passover because bookbinding glue contains ingredients that are forbidden then.

The Maccabees were not afraid of elephants or anything else.

Aunt Josie makes the *best* brisket.

The *All-of-a-Kind Family* books.

"You don't have to be Jewish to love
Levy's rye bread."

Studies have shown that chicken soup
really does help cure colds.

How 'bout those sandwiches at
the Carnegie Deli?

# Cool Things About the Bible

It's the best-selling book in the world.

Wow, look how thin the pages are.

The song "Turn, Turn, Turn"
(music by Pete Seeger) is from
the third verse of Ecclesiastes.

Exodus got turned
into a great movie.

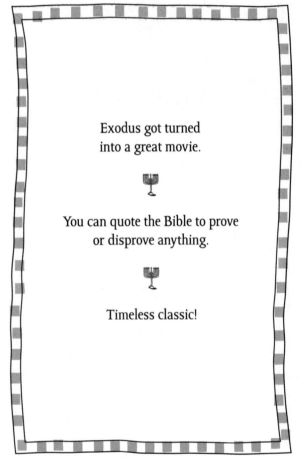

You can quote the Bible to prove
or disprove anything.

Timeless classic!

For those who enjoy math . . .
the Book of Numbers.

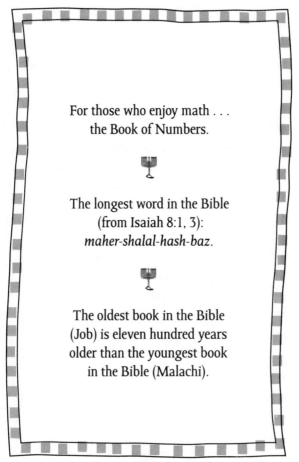

The longest word in the Bible
(from Isaiah 8:1, 3):
*maher-shalal-hash-baz*.

The oldest book in the Bible
(Job) is eleven hundred years
older than the youngest book
in the Bible (Malachi).

The longest book in the Bible is
Psalms (from the Hebrew Bible).
The shortest book in the Bible is John
(from the New Testament).

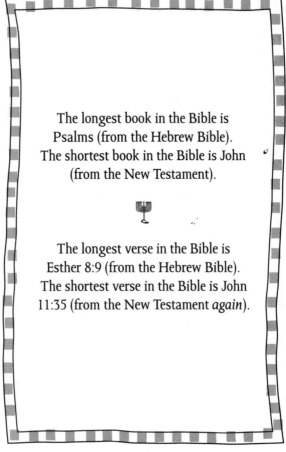

The longest verse in the Bible is
Esther 8:9 (from the Hebrew Bible).
The shortest verse in the Bible is John
11:35 (from the New Testament *again*).

Both Enoch and Elijah went to
heaven even though they never died.

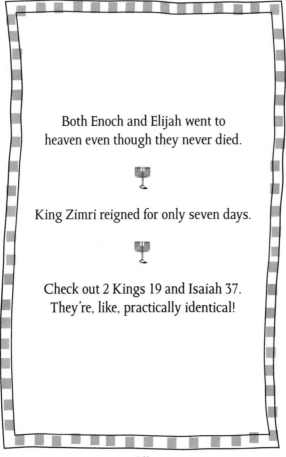

King Zimri reigned for only seven days.

Check out 2 Kings 19 and Isaiah 37.
They're, like, practically identical!

On Yom Kippur Eve, you can get a dead person's forgiveness if you ask for pardon at graveside in front of ten witnesses.

Judaism is perhaps the only major religion to attach importance to the citron.

Finally there's a ceremony to welcome girl babies *(simchat bat),* not just one for boys.

White yarmulkes on the High Holy Days!

"I have learned much from my teachers, more from
my friends, and most of all from my students."
—Rabbi Judah Ha-Nassi

Leonard Bernstein refused to enter his
dad's beauty supply business.

Irving Berlin, son of a cantor, wrote more
than a thousand songs.

Nathan Straus introduced pasteurized
milk into American schools.

✡

"Why should people be allowed to kill
animals if it is not necessary, simply
because they desire the pleasure of having
the beauty and warmth of fur coats? Is it
not possible to achieve the same degree of
warmth without fur?"
—Rabbi Chaim Dovid Helevy

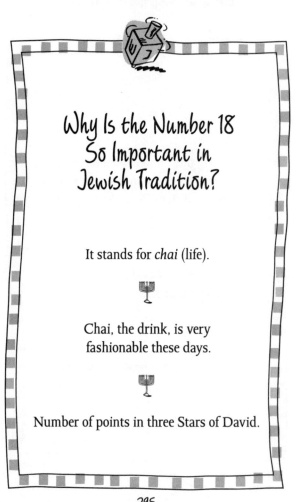

# Why Is the Number 18 So Important in Jewish Tradition?

It stands for *chai* (life).

Chai, the drink, is very fashionable these days.

Number of points in three Stars of David.

Giving money in denominations
of eighteen consoles children for having
lost the legal right to drink at eighteen.

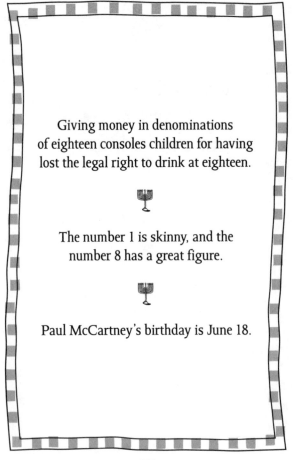

The number 1 is skinny, and the
number 8 has a great figure.

Paul McCartney's birthday is June 18.

Eighteen-wheeler trucks—so powerful!

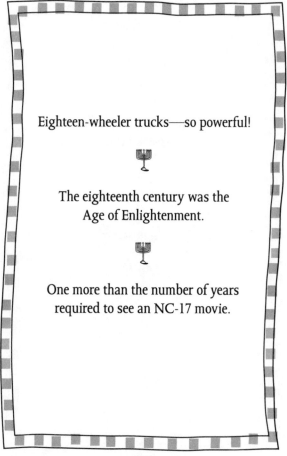

The eighteenth century was the
Age of Enlightenment.

One more than the number of years
required to see an NC-17 movie.

Number of players on
two baseball teams.

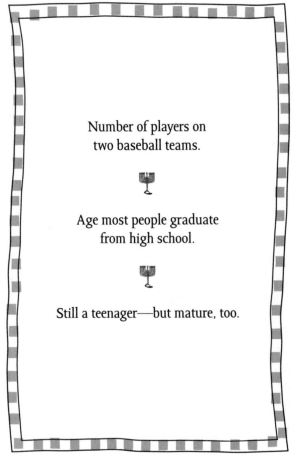

Age most people graduate
from high school.

Still a teenager—but mature, too.

Judaism doesn't have the
concept of religious celibacy.

Rugulach would be nowhere without us.

Likewise, prune lekvar.

No fasting required during Lent or Ramadan.

You get to use a noisemaker on Purim.

One of us must've invented kosher dill pickles.

✡

(And one of us did invent Levi's.)

✡

Dick Cavett: "Are you a Jew?"
Jonathan Miller: "Jew-ish."

✡

When an aspiring writer sent Benjamin
Disraeli a manuscript to review, his reply was:
"Dear Sir, I thank you for sending me a copy of
your book, which I shall waste no time in reading."

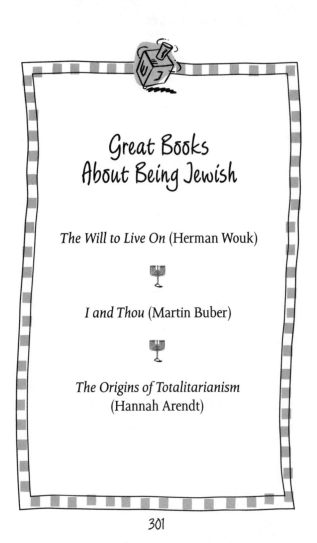

# Great Books
# About Being Jewish

*The Will to Live On* (Herman Wouk)

*I and Thou* (Martin Buber)

*The Origins of Totalitarianism*
(Hannah Arendt)

*The Melting Pot Drama in Four Acts*
(Israel Zangwill)

*Painted Bird* (Jerzy Kosinski)

*The Periodic Table* (Primo Levi)

*Tevye's Daughters and Other Stories*
(Sholem Aleichem)

*The Fixer* (Bernard Malamud)

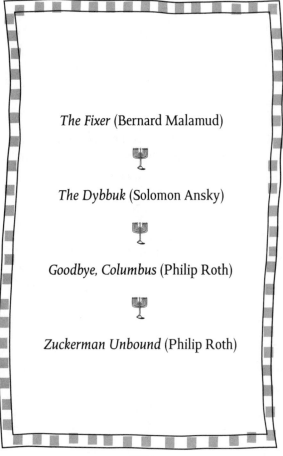

*The Dybbuk* (Solomon Ansky)

*Goodbye, Columbus* (Philip Roth)

*Zuckerman Unbound* (Philip Roth)

Did you know that Alfred Dreyfus of the famed
Dreyfus Affair is a distant relative of Richard
Dreyfus and Julia Louis-Dreyfus?

Rebecca was judged suitable to be a wife
of the patriarch Isaac because of her kindness
in giving water to the ten camels of Eliezer,
Abraham's servant.

You get their holidays off,
but they don't get yours.

Everyone knows that kosher hot dogs rule.

"I once wanted to be an atheist but I gave up . . .
they have no holidays." —Henny Youngman

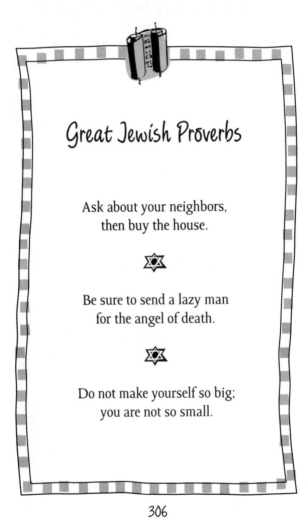

# Great Jewish Proverbs

Ask about your neighbors,
then buy the house.

✡

Be sure to send a lazy man
for the angel of death.

✡

Do not make yourself so big;
you are not so small.

Do not meet troubles halfway.

Don't be too sweet lest you be eaten up;
don't be too sour lest you be spewed out.

Don't make a mountain out of a molehill.

Don't look a gift horse in the mouth.

Don't make a toil of pleasure.

Don't pick a wasp out of a cream-jug.
(*Huh?*)

God gives burdens—also shoulders.

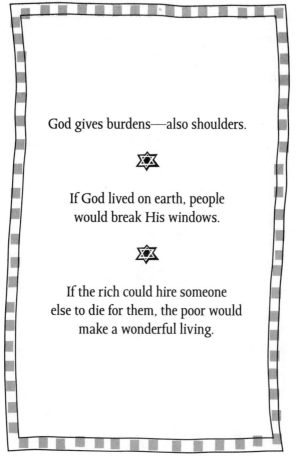

If God lived on earth, people
would break His windows.

If the rich could hire someone
else to die for them, the poor would
make a wonderful living.

If you can't go over, you must go under.

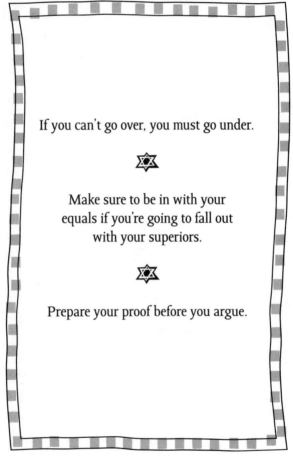

Make sure to be in with your
equals if you're going to fall out
with your superiors.

Prepare your proof before you argue.

The innkeeper loves a drunkard,
but not for a son-in-law.

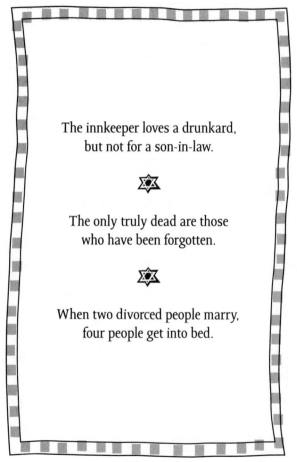

The only truly dead are those
who have been forgotten.

When two divorced people marry,
four people get into bed.

Who teases you loves you.

✡

With money in your pocket
you are wise, you are handsome,
and you sing well, too.

✡

Your friend has a friend; don't tell him.
(*Huh?*)

Don't mess with Uncle Morris:
He fought in the Israeli army.

A Chanukah bush is a lot easier to
bring home than a Christmas tree.

Nobody minds if you talk during the service.
Or even leave.

Q: How many Jewish mothers does it
take to screw in a lightbulb?
A: (Sigh.) Don't bother. I'll sit in the dark.
I don't want to be a nuisance to anybody.

Next year in Jerusalem!